oronto printers' strike followed by rade Union Act

ominion Lands Act Homesteading Act)

Amor de Cosmos premier of British Columbia

1873

rince Edward Island joins Confederation as 7th province

Canadian Labour Union organized

Indian Treaty #3 with Ojibway

Louis Riel elected M.P. for Provencher, Manitoba

Winnipeg incorporated as a city

Grip established by J.W. Bengough

Pacific Scandal; Macdonald resigns November 6; Alexander Mackenzie takes over power as head of Reform-Liberals

"ISN'T THAT A DAINTY DISH TO SET BEFORE A KING?"—NURSERY RHYME.

Cypress Hills Massacre

North-West Mounted Police established

First North American golf club established in Montreal

Daniel O'Donoghue first trade unionist elected to office as M.P.

Fort Erie International Bridge completed

World-wide depression

Wreck of the *Atlantic* off Ha 560 lives lost

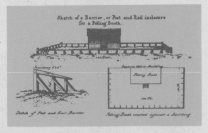

1874

Royal Military College established in Kingston

Ontario Education Act: school compulsory for children aged seven to twelve

Ontario School of Agriculture opens in Guelph

Trial of Ambroise Lépine for Scott execution

The *Nation* established by Canada First

THE **NATION.**

ilies
ba

Indian Treaty #4 with Cree and Ojibway

Federal Election confirms Mackenzie as P.M.

Election Act establishes secret ballot and single-day voting

Carnarvon Arbitration between Dominion and B.C. over CPR

Decision on Guibord case rendered by English Privy Council

First international football match: McGill vs. Harvard

First intercollegiate football match: Queen's vs. Varsity

The Age of Innocence

Singing the National Anthem at Midnight Leaving Sarnia

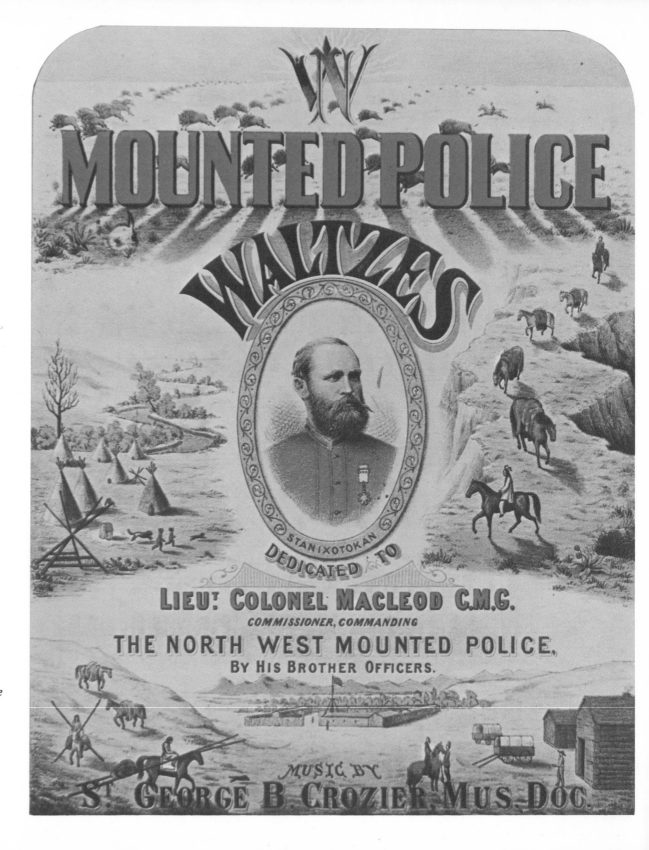

Long before "Rose Marie," the North-West Mounted Police became the subject of romantic literature and the inspiration of composers. These waltzes were dedicated to Stanixotokan (Bull's Head), the Blackfoot name for J.F. Macleod.

Robert Collins
The Age of Innocence
1870/1880

Canada's Illustrated Heritage

Canada's Illustrated Heritage

Publisher: Jack McClelland
Editorial Consultant: Pierre Berton
Historical Consultant: Michael Bliss
Editor-in-Chief: Toivo Kiil
Associate Editors: Clare McKeon
Jean Stinson
Designer: David Shaw
Cover Artist: Alan Daniel
Picture Research: William Bilecki
Lembi Buchanan
Judy Forman
Betty Gibson
Patricia McLoughlin

ISBN: 0-9196-4419-8

N.S.L. Natural Science of Canada Limited
254 Bartley Drive
Toronto, Ontario M4A 1G4

Printed and bound in Canada

PROGRAMME.

ROCKWELL & STONE'S
MAMMOTH
CIRCUS.
FOR ONE NIGHT ONLY.

TORONTO, WEDNESDAY EV'G, AUG. 26.

PROPRIETORS,	ROCKWELL & STONE.
EQUESTRIAN MANAGER,	HENRY NEEDHAM.
ACTING MANAGER,	WILLIAM HUBBELL.
CLOWNS,	JOHN GOSSIN & BOB WILLIAMS.
RING MASTER,	F. WHITTAKER.
TREASURER,	E. G. MEAD.

Performances will open with the

TOURNAMENT ENTREE.

DOG BUFFER
Will be introduced by his Master, BOB WILLIAMS.

DOUBLE LEAPS OVER VARIOUS OBJECTS
BY H. FRANKLIN.

Ground and Lofty Tumbling
By the entire strength of the Company.

THE ARENA'S PRIDE, ON HER PALFREY,
MRS. GOSSIN.

HORSE COLUMBUS
will be instructed by his Master, F. WHITTAKER.

JUVENILE WONDER,
Master STEVENS, in his admired Single Horse Act.

The Unapproachable
FRANKLIN, ON THE CORDE VOLANTE

A Laughable Equestrian Scene,
By J. GOSSIN & CHAMPION.

A new Scene on the
TIGHT ROPE, by the accomplished HERR CLINE.

Groups and Posies,
By those talented Artistes, FRANKLIN & STEVENS.

THE CHAMPION OF THE ARENA,
LEVI NORTH, in a daring Equestrian Act.

MUSCULAR AND DARING FEATS,
By the Modern Sampson, ALONZA HUBBLE.

The Diversions to close with the Magnificent and Original Spanish Pageant, the
BULL FIGHT, or Spanish Games of Olden Times.

☞ First Class Seats, 2s. 6d. ;—Second Class Seats, 1s. 3d. ;—
Children, under 10, half price.—Open at 7 ;—to commence at 7¼.
☞ Females not admitted unless accompanied by a Gentleman.

J. CLELAND, PRINTER.

Contents

By its tenth birthday, July 1, 1877, the young nation encompassed seven provinces, each romantically symbolized here by an artist for L'Opinion Publique.

This Thing Called Nationhood

The future of Canada depends very largely upon the cultivation of a national spirit.

Edward Blake, "Aurora Speech," 1873

They are only a grandfather's step behind us, those Canadians of the 1870s, but their country is as strange and remote as some distant galaxy. True, the place names are ones we all know. The people's worries, too, are remarkably like ours: how to live on a meagre income, how to stay healthy, how to keep the children from turning into delinquents. And in the decade's happenings – new ideas in retailing, the beginnings of mechanized farming, the first true labour unions, the humbling of the proud Indian – are many of the seeds of today. It is a time of awakening, the first timid awareness of a changing world, the first halting steps of a new nation.

But so far, these are merely stirrings. Mostly, this is a quaint, unrecognizable Canada: only four provinces, as the decade begins; only three more, by the end, and the North-West Territories a vast sweep of wilderness and prairie. The population hovers around four million, three-quarters of it in Ontario and Quebec. Nearly all the people, even in the cities, are very close to the forest, land or sea. This is a rustic Canada.

Every port, coastal or inland, is clotted with sails and masts. Among the Maritime villages, nets lie thick as cobwebs on the grass. In Halifax the twenty-nine thousand people brag about their fish market with sixteen different species, more than any other in North America. Montreal, by far the largest city with one hundred and fifteen thousand people, is really just two oversized towns, French and English, stitched together by St. Lawrence Main Street. "They move along parallel lines, neither affecting the other," says a contemporary writer. "There is no fusion of races in commercial, social or political life; the differences are sharply defined and appear to be permanent."

Downtown Montreal gets flooded every spring, like any backwoods village (there'll be no St. Lawrence River breakwater for another ten years) and the entire city is about to be swamped in waves of derision from abroad. In 1875 poet Samuel Butler arrives from England to discover the famed *Discobolus,* a Greek statue of a discus thrower, banished to a storeroom in the Montreal Natural History Society museum. The statue of the naked athlete is, to the Society, vulgar. Butler pens his famous refrain "O God! O Montreal!" and Canada's intellectuals squirm.

The nation's capital is a muddy town with forest pressing in on its flanks. Lady Dufferin, the new governor general's wife, cocks her pretty Irish snoot at Ottawa's "incongruously beautiful buildings crowning its insignificance. A very bad road leads to Rideau Hall. . . . The house appears to me to be at the land's end."

John B. Shelden of Millville, N.J., claimed to have discovered the North Pole on the 25th of October, 1869. According to his description, "the Pole is a topaz or diamond. The water around the Pole never freezes. The outer wall is ice."

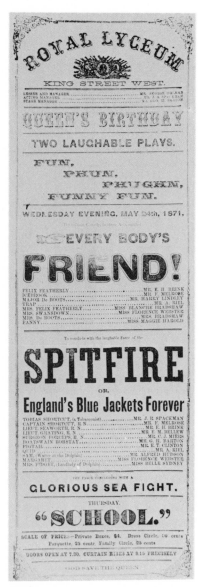

Tickets for the "fun phun phugn funny fun" farces at Toronto's Royal Lyceum ranged from $4.00 for a private box to 25¢ in the family circle.

Herds of cattle plod to market along Toronto's Front Street. Winnipeg is a bleak huddle of frame shanties, three hundred people, and parallel tracks of Red River carts running west to infinity. Those tracks lead travellers through an ocean of grass, scrub poplar, willows and coulees; among Cree, Assiniboine, Blackfoot, Métis, priests and traders; finally, after two weeks' ride, civilization – Edmonton – a fort!

Over the mountains there is no Vancouver and won't be in this decade; its predecessor, Gastown (soon to be Granville), is a clutter of shacks around a saloon on Burrard Inlet. Only Victoria, of all the Canadian cities, does not cause well-bred visiting Britishers to shudder. Here you can buy a piano, hire a chimney-sweep or plant roses with reasonable assurance they won't be trampled by stray cows or buffalo. Victoria has even brought its fist fights indoors, with sparring exhibitions of "muscular Christianity" every Tuesday and Saturday nights in Armstrong's Old Lager Beer Cellar.

sights and sounds

So this is still a somewhat primitive Canada, but its sights, sounds, tastes and smells are all the more tantalizing. At night the lamplighter trudges city streets with his taper, leaving flickering gaslight in his wake. By day the bricklayer, hod on shoulder, moves patiently up and down his ladder, building walls by inches. Around him the streets throng with carts and carriages; gentlemen in frock-coats, stovepipe hats and enough whiskers to make the weakest face look like officer material; women with their stomachs laced to the point of agony, their backs arched, their bottoms extended with bustles and their ankle-length skirts whispering over the boardwalks.

The walk or drive is a favourite entertainment, as is dancing until sun-up and eating to the verge of apoplexy. This is a fine country for eating.

Oysters come from the coasts by barrelsful. Lobsters flop in the shallows of the Miramichi River with every outgoing tide; you can buy a hundred for fifty cents. The daily bill of fare at Toronto's St. Nicholas restaurant lists seventy-one items. Food is cheap – and different. The bread is gritty from rough milling. Eggs taste gamey because hens run free to eat bugs. Milk is tainted with turnips, wild herbs or stinkweed. Sugar has a molasses flavour. Only an iron-clad stomach can escape what one Canadian magazine calls "our national dyspepsia."

gentle to the ear

This is no place for a delicate nose, either. The backcountry is fragrant with sawdust, fresh-turned sod and smouldering brush, but the cities stink of uncovered garbage, outdoor privies, horse manure, people who never take baths, and people who wear Bearine ("Prepared from pure bear's grease! Makes the hair soft, pliant and glossy and is delightful to use. Only 50¢").

And the sounds? Well, even the language has a strange cadence. The written word moves ponderously, magnificently, like a royal barge: "Tomorrow I shall hasten to the presence of her from whom I hope I may never henceforth be parted" and "His attendants were paragons of kindness, celerity and attention." The spoken word is full of "fixin's" (almost any kind of ad-lib cookery), "sanguine" (optimistic) people, and such homespun phrases as "I calculate them apples'll want regulatin' soon" (Translation: "I think those apples that are drying in the sun should be turned over"). "In pronouncing, if you would imitate a Canadian," writes a visiting Englishman, "you would need to open your mouth very wide and make as much of each sound as you can."

Generally, though, the seventies are gentle to the ear. There are great open spaces of silence, punctuated only by the clip-clop of hooves, hiss of sleigh runners, thunk of axe, and the melody of sleighbells, churchbells, cowbells. There is, to be sure, the railway train, a raucous wonder clanging and charging all over the East at incredible speeds of twenty to thirty miles per hour. But the rattle of wheels, along roads alternately gooey with mud or grey with dust, is a more familiar sound. Roads are still essential lifelines and Canadians gratefully await the "roadmaker" – the first frost. Roads, rails and water carry people, mail, goods and routine news. Only important messages and important people use Mr. Morse's telegraph, the lines being extended during these years to Edmonton. Ordinary people and things move leisurely. And why not? Life is short, too short to be taken at the dead run.

And yet science and invention are gradually changing these simple ways. Elevators are coming into office buildings, enabling them to be built higher than four or five storeys, which is as much stair-climbing as people will tolerate. Farm machinery is getting efficient and complicated with gears, levers and drive-wheels.

"Yes, Alex, it is I"

On an August day in 1876 Alexander Bell picks up his crude telephone in Paris, Ontario, and hears a voice on the wire: "Yes, Alex, it is I, your father, speaking from Brantford!" On a May evening two years later Lady Dufferin tells her diary, "This morning we had an exhibition of the phonograph. Two men brought this wonderful invention for us to see. It is quite a small thing, a cylinder which you turn with a handle, and which you place on a common table. We were so amazed when we first heard this bit of iron speak that it was hard to believe there was no trick!"

And in the last days of the decade, Montrealers go home with the *Monetary Times,* strike a

"lucifer" match with its whiff of sulphur, pull up to the kerosene lamp and read, "Mr. Edison at last claims to have perfected the electric light and he intends to illuminate with it the houses in the hamlet where he lives. Holders of gas shares will look on the public test of Christmas Eve with some degree of anxiety."

There are other more pressing anxieties in the seventies. One of them is sheer everyday survival: the dread of diseases that medicine can neither prevent nor cure; the terror of fires that race through whole ramshackle city blocks long before the lumbering horse-drawn fire wagons can reach the scene.

Another worry is the new thing called nationhood. Most Canadians are, of course, very loyal to Queen and Empire. Stout fellows everywhere still spring instantly to their feet to offer three cheers for Her Majesty, His Excellency, the commanding general or almost anybody. Who could feel anything but affection for kindly, dumpy, middle-aged Victoria, already on the throne longer than most Canadians can remember? But she and the British Army (recently shipped back home) are ten or twelve days away by steamship, longer by sail. Confederation is only three years old. Quebec, not only wary of its fellow provinces, is also warring within itself: conservative and liberal factions inside the Roman Catholic Church are diametrically opposed to one another.

Still, the country is hanging together. More and more, Canadians realize they are on their own, with a strong belligerent neighbour next door. Little by little, they become aware of and are often baffled by other parts of their land but the awareness is at least a start. They are beginning to think of themselves not only as Ontarians, Maritimers or Québecois but something more. Maybe even that nation-from-sea-to-sea that the Fathers dreamed about and the people wanted but didn't really understand.

The centre of cultural activities in any city was the opera house. The new Grand Opera House opened in 1874 with Sheridan's The School for Scandal, *starring Mrs. Morrison, the proprietor, as Lady Teazle.*

Main Street, Canada

Forests of masts in the ocean ports, horse-drawn wagons on muddy streets, wooden sidewalks and porticos, gas-lit thoroughfares and street railways – these were the characteristics of Main Street, Canada, where merchants displayed their wares and elegant couples promenaded amongst bowler-hatted businessmen in the age of innocence.

Horses and carts lined the sidewalks of Halifax's Bedford Row on market day, a day not only for conducting business but also for greeting old friends and catching up on the news.

Below: *St. John's, Newfoundland, heart of the colony that would hold aloof from Confederation for eighty years.*

Breakneck Steps leading up from Quebec City's historic Lower Town was a favourite spot for shoppers and photographers in the 1870s.

And on the far Pacific Coast, the hardy citizens of Victoria, so recently a fort, revelled in the signs of civilization as their year of Confederation approached.

Toronto's King Street East was the place to see and be seen parading in one's finest of an afternoon.

CHAPTER ONE

Curling, Curtsies and Good, Clean Fun

There are few sights more beautiful than that of a pretty girl gyrating on her silver sandals.

Canadian Illustrated News, December 30, 1871

The Montreal outing of Christmas Day 1875 was, as the *Canadian Illustrated News* put it, "a most delightful entertainment." It had everything a well-bred, fun-loving Canadian could possibly want: food, dancing, fresh air, pretty women, gallant officers and fine horseflesh. It was the annual "drive" of Lt. Col. Frank Bond, commander of the Prince of Wales Rifles, a towering fellow with a voice like cannon thunder. When Colonel Bond ran a drive, sir, it was organized like a jolly good war.

Sharp at three o'clock on that bitter sunny Saturday, sixty sleighs, cutters and carrioles with high curly runners and prancing ponies assembled in Dominion Square. At the reins were gentlemen in military greatcoats, wedge-shaped fur hats, fiercely bristling moustaches, their backs as straight as rifle barrels. Beside them huddled the ladies in fur muffs and hats, under buffalo or bearskin robes, their feet toasting on hot bricks or hot-water warmers, their doe-like eyes and little rosebud mouths buried in blue, pink or green "clouds" – the woollen scarves that were standard winter equipment for every Canadian woman.

They lined up for photographers, then jingle-jangled along Sherbrooke Street and down St. James, through snowy canyons formed by man-high banks shovelled to either sidewalk, and six miles through the vast, white, lung-searing countryside to Longue Pointe. God help any young officer who slowed down; the Colonel permitted no lagging. The drive "effectually dispelled any lurking spirit of melancholy."

Longue Pointe Hotel was bedecked with evergreen wreaths and coloured lanterns. Off came the wraps, revealing a rainbow of tunics and gowns. Up the receiving line went each guest to shake the Colonel's hand; then onto the dance floor where Herr Gruenwald's orchestra was offering waltzes, polkas and minuets. For two hours they danced with untiring zeal, stopping frequently for ice cream and lemonade. Sharp at 7:30 P.M. the Colonel marched them into the dining room. Supper was a heaping little snack of chicken, beef, oysters, ham and lobster. Then back to the dance with increased vigour until ten o'clock; finally the "scamper home through the clear frosty night."

The drive was not lower-class entertainment (clerks and labourers just couldn't afford a horse and rig), but its basic simplicity was the essence of all good Canadian fun. Daily life was lean and spare – work hard, raise a family, fear God, revere the Queen – and pleasures were equally straightforward, whether the dance was jig or minuet and the supper, meat pie or oysters.

Canada's belle of the rink was Lady Dufferin. By the end of her first year in Canada, she could perform "the outside edge backwards."

Opposite page: The highlight of the winter season was the fancy-dress skating ball when Montreal society turned out in splendiferous costumes to trip the light fantastic on skates.

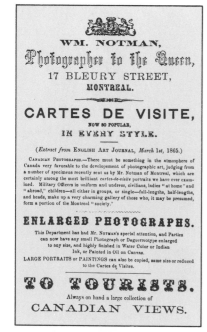

Visiting Cards

"Leaving a card with the corner bent
signifies that it was left by its owner
in person, not sent by a servant.
Bending the edges of a card means
that the visit was designed for the
young ladies of the house, . . . and a
visit may be from five minutes to
half an hour, never longer unless
with a very intimate friend."

*The Canadian Home
Cook Book, 1877*

It was a time of *doing* rather than *watching*.
Spectator sports were just beginning to develop in
Canada and, because privacy was not yet a luxury
and the pioneer yearning for human fellowship was
still strong, people sought their entertainment *en
masse*. Like all things Victorian, fun was expected
to follow specific rules. The earlier practice of
conversing in booming voices – orating, really – at
social gatherings was now a mark of the oaf.
Canadians who followed their etiquette books
suppressed "undue emotion whether of laughter,
anger, mortification, disappointment or selfish-
ness." No gentleman ever stared at his pocket-
watch, uninvited, in polite society. No lady appeared in public without gloves. No man left home
without his engraved calling cards, any more than
he left without his pants. No lady worthy of the
name ever used such profanity as "the dickens" or
"mercy!"

It was the time of curtsies, bows and "calls"
(between noon and 5:00 P.M. for congratulations,
condolences or simple friendship). The "cut" was a
way of discouraging advances or dropping former
friends: not to return a bow was a gentle cut; a
vicious cut was a long silent stare. It was a time
when ladies were expected to be coy, and fluttering
eyelids half-hidden behind a fan signified "You
may speak to me." It was a time when no man
failed to bow if his glance met a lady's eyes, and
when it was "the duty of gentlemen to do all that
they can to make the occasion enjoyable and even
mirthful."

The most abundant source of mirth was outdoors. In even the largest cities, the country was
only minutes away. Hordes of muscular young
men in toques, wool coats, moccasins and gay
sashes plodded through the night on snowshoes by
the light of coal-oil torches. Whole families from

*High necklines, long sleeves and full-length flounced skirts with bustles could not be abandoned even for a croquet
game on a warm summer afternoon at Belmere in Quebec's Eastern Townships.*

Winnipeg to Nova Scotia went curling on open ponds (in this decade proper curling stones were first imported from Scotland). Skiing was unknown in Canada but everyone tobogganned, especially in Montreal. The sledders coasted down Peel Street, Mount Royal (officially made a park in 1876), Côte des Neiges or, as settlement reached out, down hills that later became Mountain Street and Clarke Avenue.

The winter mania was ice skating. Every living soul of walking age strapped on the blades, from the blacksmith and his wife to Lord and Lady Dufferin. The handsome governor general was an indefatigable good sport. During his 1872-78 term he travelled to every corner of Canada by every conveyance from paddle steamer to stage coach, often with his pretty Irish wife at his side. At home or on state visits, both found time to skate every winter day and Lady Dufferin proudly told her diary, "D. can go backwards and do the figure of eight."

The skating *tour de force* of the Dufferins' years was a Montreal costume ball. Montrealers were justly proud of the new Victoria Rink on Drummond Street, one of the finest and biggest in the world. Its seventeen-thousand-square-foot ice surface was surrounded by a promenade platform and orchestra gallery and was lit by five thousand gas jets shining through coloured glass globes. Here on January 30, 1873, the Dufferins watched hundreds of skaters cavort about as Indians, mandarins, cavaliers and monkeys. Then, for the visitors' benefit, skilful couples danced "the lancers" and "Sir Roger de Coverley" on skates. Finally Dufferin himself stepped out and only by playing "God Save the Queen" did they eventually get the enthusiastic governor general to go home.

Enthusiasm – that was the operative word in

Madame Albani
The Voice of Empire

Prima donna of prima donnas, Marie Louise Emma Cécile Lajeunesse, was born at Chambly, Quebec, studied in Albany, N.Y. (whence her stage name) and in Paris and Milan. Audiences cheered the 23-year-old soprano at her 1870 Italian debut in Bellini's *La Sonnambula,* and she continued to thrill royalty and concert-goers in the great opera houses of the world until her retirement in 1906. Then, after losing her fortune in the stock market, she tried a new career in English music halls. She died in poverty in 1930, but the recordings she made in 1904-5 live on as collector's items today.

By the 1870s, the sewing machine had made the preparation of specialized clothing easier, and the elaborate white wedding gown suitable only for that one special day became the dictate of fashion.

Mr. Notman's Fashionable Society

The outstanding photographer of Canada's Victorian era, William Notman (left) opened his first Montreal studio in 1856. By the 1870s he had branches in Ottawa, Halifax, Toronto and Boston. In the forefront of every technical advance and photographic fad, the Scotsman had an artist's instinct for the most flattering lighting for the subjects he posed amid impressive props. Held rigidly in position by ingenious supports, politicians and royalty, the famous and the fashionable endured the 60-second exposure time for the decade's status symbol – a portrait by Notman, "Photographer to the Queen."

The full crinoline-supported skirt of the '60s gave way in 1870 to a slimmer front line but lots of material pulled to the sides and back over a bustle.

By mid-decade the "new" bustle had reached exaggerated proportions. Pleats, flounces and lace and ribbon trimming showed off the dressmaker's skills.

In fur-trimmed basque-style coat designed for wearing over a bustled dress, this beauty was ready for winter.

In lacy pantalettes, the youngest posed wearily against Sister, the mini-image of mama right up to the earrings.

The modified "cutaway" suit in a light-coloured, fine check, with only one coat button fastenable, marked the height of male fashion in the '70s. The silk top hat was still mandatory.

A member of the Montreal Bicycle Club, formed in 1878, takes pride in the differential gears of his tricycle, an exotic predecessor of the two-wheeled safety bicycle of 1885.

Canada. Everyone became involved, even in the budding spectator sports. When small-town gangs such as the Forty Fighting Coopers of Churchville or Port Credit's five Sharp brothers (each over six-foot-four) met periodically for fist fights, the onlookers generally ended up cracking heads too. There were no sports stadiums, so when teams played – the Gentlemen, famous touring cricketers from England; the Toronto Dauntless baseball club; the Caughnawaga Indian lacrosse team; the first international football match, Harvard against McGill in 1874 – spectators crowded the sidelines in frock-coats and mutton-chop whiskers, cheering raucously and dodging stray balls or hurtling bodies. When Ned Hanlan, the sensational sculler, rowed in Toronto harbour, hero-worshipping fans tagged along the sidelines in rowboats.

It was a time of challenges and sidebets, in everything from horse-racing to billiards. Here, in an 1877 issue of the *Canadian Gentleman's Journal & Sporting Times*, J.L. O'Connor of Oakville stands ready to outjump any man in Ontario for $1,000. Here, too, is Joe Labossière of Quebec City, six-foot-one and 210 pounds, challenging any man in Canada to a glove fight for $500. And here is artilleryman Ambrose Carney, six-foot-three, 200 pounds and a "student of the science of boxing" under one Professor Woods, coming on to beat Labossière in three bloody rounds.

the people cheered

There were plays, minstrel shows, lectures, band concerts and circuses ("Now hurry-hurry-hurry, two performing tents of living wild animals from the almost impenetrable jungles of Asia and Bengal and the dark caves of Ethiopia.") There were parades for politicians, royalty and fraternal orders, usually under street arches of flowers, slogans or a city's favourite products, whether they were chairs or cheese. These were all live flesh-

and-blood entertainments to see, hear, touch or smell, and the people always cheered and clapped.

Even if you hadn't a cent, there was no need to be bored. Grown-ups contentedly spent entire evenings at whist, checkers, billiards, Parcheesi or cribbage. Every group had an amateur conjuror, or soloist, or reader of Tennyson, or enactor of tableaux. It was not uncommon to see a roomful of adults in their Sunday best capering through a game of blind-man's-buff: indeed, it was one of the few ways a man could legally lay hands on a pretty girl.

a Saturday afternoon stroll

Anyone from clerk to colonel could indulge in the afternoon walk and nearly everyone did, all combed, brushed and dressed in their finest. "Picture to yourself," said a writer describing the Saturday afternoon stroll down Montreal's St. James street, "a double stream of people flowing on each side of the street, a tide that almost overflows the sidewalks. People are marching abreast in groups of three or four when they can, usually in twos, as in the ranks of a procession or convoy; or often, one after the other, like ducks on their way to the river."

Country people liked to combine their pleasure with business. Corn-husking was an opportunity for "sparking"; a man finding a red kernel (not difficult in those days of Indian corn) was entitled to kiss the girl of his choice and if he was shy she might just flick a kernel his way. At apple-paring time, a girl could toss a curly peeling over her shoulder to see if it formed an initial – a clue to her future husband. A logging or barn-raising bee, where whisky flowed free, was certain to end in a dance and at least one fist fight, both bona fide sports.

Dancing was a foot-stomping, bottom-pinching free-for-all in the country and a rule-abiding ritual

LACROSSE! LACROSSE!
The National Game of Canada.

TWELVE CANADIAN GENTLEMEN
v.
TWELVE IROQUOIS INDIANS.

HER MOST GRACIOUS MAJESTY

THE QUEEN

Having commanded the Canadian Lacrosse Teams to

PLAY BEFORE THE ROYAL FAMILY

At Windsor, on Monday, June 26th, their appearance on the

LONGSIGHT

CRICKET GROUND

IS POSTPONED TO

TUESDAY AND WEDNESDAY,
JUNE 27th and 28th, 1876.

The following are the names of the Players :--

CANADIANS.	IROQUOIS INDIANS.	
Captain - Dr. Wm. Geo. Beers	Tier Karoniare	alias Blue Spotted
Gaol - H. Wylie Becket	Aton8aTekanennao8iheu	„ Hickory Wood Split
Point - G. S. Hubbell	Sha8atis Anasotako	„ Pick the Feather
Coverpoint - S. Massey	Sha8atis Aientonni	„ Hole in the Sky
Centre - S. Struthers	8ishe Taienontii	„ Flying Name
Field - D. E. Bowie	Aton1a Teronko8a	„ The Loon
„ - T. G. Hodgson	8ishe Ononsanoron	„ Deer House
„ - W. O. Ross	Saksarrii Tontariiakon	„ Crossing the River
„ - Angus Grant	Tier Skanenrati	„ Outside the Multitude
„ - J. Summerhayes	Rasar Kanentakeron	„ Scattered Branches
Home - T. G. Ralston	Kor Kanentakeron	„ Spruce Branches
„ - F. M'Indoe	Saksarii Shokosennakete	„ Great Arm
„ - G. T. R. Greene	Alon8a Ton8nnata	„ Wild Wind
„ - H. Joseph		
„ - S. MacDonald		

POSITIVELY THEIR FINAL APPEARANCE
IN ENGLAND.

Play to Commence each day at 3 o'clock.

The cricket lawns of Britain were the scene of the first international demonstration of lacrosse, billed as "Canada's national game" by its promoter, Dr. George Beers. In 1860 he had developed rules for an organized version of the Indian game "baggataway." The Iroquois Indians listed on the poster were the famed Caughnawaga team.

1793. YORK PIONEERS. 1871.

THE SECOND
GRAND DINNER
IN THE ST. LAWRENCE HALL,
MONDAY APRIL 17, 1871,
AT 6 O'CLOCK, P.M.

BILL OF FARE.

SOUPS.
MOCK TURTLE.   OYSTER.

FISH.
SALM IN TROUT,   CODFISH,
Anchovy Sauce.   Oyster Sauce.

ENTREES.
RIZ DE VEAU,   COTELETTES D'AGNEAU,
On Petit Pois.   Champignons.
COTELETTES DE VENISON, PETITE PATES D'HUITRES,
Sauce on Vin.
VOL-AU-VENT D'HOMARD. COTELETTE DE VEAU,
                      Sauce Tomati.

ROAST.
SIRLOIN BEEF,   PORK,   LAMB,   SADDLE OF MUTTON,
Horse Radish. Apple Sauce. Mint Sauce. Currant Jelly.
CHICKENS.   TURKEY.

BOILED.
ROUND CORNED BEEF.   LEG OF MUTTON,
                            Caper Sauce.
HAMS.   TONGUES.

VEGETABLES.
POTATOES.   TURNIPS.   CARROTS.   ARTICHOKES.

SECOND COURSE.
ROAST WILD DUCK.   ROAST PRAIRIE FOWL.   ITALIAN SALAD.
PLUM PUDDING,   CABINET PUDDING,
Brandy Sauce.   Wine Sauce.

PASTRY.
APPLE.   PLUM.   PEACH.   STRAWBERRY.   RHUBARB.
CHARLOTTE RUSSE.   ITALIEN CREAM.   RUM FRENCH JELLY.
NEUGAT.   WINE JELLY.   BLANCMANGE.   TIPSEY CAKE.

CELERY.   RADISHES.   BUTTER.   CHEESE.
WINE—PORT AND SHERRY.   HOT PUNCH AND BEER.

W. STEER, Caterer.

The York Pioneers, a Toronto Historical Society, offered a cornucopia of culinary delights for their 1871 Grand Dinner.

in the city. No city girl dared speak to a strange man even if they ended up face to face in a minuet. No city male dared press a lady's waist during the waltz; only a touch with the open palm. Yet no book of manners concerned itself with the overpowering male aroma of stale sweat, cigars and chewing tobacco which rose to heady heights during a dance. A little honest body odour didn't seem to embarrass friends or lovers. Indeed some books warned girls to beware of the scented dandy; he was probably disguising some *real* evil, like bad teeth.

Most parents allowed dancing for older children as long as it was thoroughly chaperoned. But nice girls never went unescorted or attended *public* dance halls. Far better that young people spend their spare time in useful toil such as picking berries, or harmless fun such as spelling bees, taffy pulls or hay rides. Parents didn't seem to realize that the prime attraction of the last event was the delicious possibility of being dumped in the hay or a snowdrift, and getting a chance to brush against the opposite sex. Maybe even hold hands! Or sneak a kiss!

Dances, interspersed with heaping meals, sometimes lasted until dawn. By then it was time for breakfast which, in the experience of one visitor to Montreal, was "a multitude of little oval dishes on which were fish, steaks, chops, ham, chicken, turkey, rissoles, potatoes (boiled, roast and fried) cabbage, corn, cheese, onions and pickles, besides plates of hot rolls, buns, crumpets, toast and biscuits, flanked by a great jug full of milk and an enormous vessel of coffee."

Such gargantuan feasts were, in themselves, recognized pleasures in the seventies. Whole evenings were dedicated to eating oysters shipped in barrels from the East Coast. Whole days were devoted to picnics. A suggested list of provisions for a forty-person picnic began: "Joint of cold roast beef, joint of cold boiled beef, two ribs of lamb, two shoulders of lamb, four roast fowls, two roast ducks, one ham, one tongue, two veal and ham pies, two pigeon pies, six medium-size lobsters. . . ." It went on and on through salads, fruit, biscuits, cheesecakes, turnovers, puddings, pies, ale, lemonade, sherry, claret, champagne and brandy.

But you got *hungry* from the footraces, archery, croquet, baseball and swimming. Why, the girl-watching alone could put a fierce edge on the appetite, all those ravishing creatures in swimsuits of sailor blouse, long skirt and longer bloomers. ("Ned! Hey Ned! I can see her ankles!") Anyway, the long jolting ride home was guaranteed to shake down the heartburn. And for the gentle sex there was always one compensating, comfortable thought. A lady always knew, never doubted that the gentlemen would provide "the means of conveyance to and from the spot selected for the festivities and make such arrangements as are necessary in the way of providing music, games and whatever else is needed to enhance the pleasure of the day."

SPORTING TIMES

The age of innocence was a decade of firsts in Canadian sports –
first world champion oarsman, first organized hockey game,
first international and intercollegiate football games, first North
American golf club, first bicycle club and first tennis
tournament. And newspapers, scrambling to cover the scene, first established
the post of "sporting editor." But they didn't try to
compete with that marvellous repository of challenges and wagers,
P.F. Collins' *The Canadian Gentleman's Journal and Sporting Times.*

Canada's Ned Hanlan defeats U.S. champion, Fred Plaisted, on Toronto Bay in 1878.

Challenges and Wagers

Although these players probably posed individually in a studio, open-air curling was the norm in the seventies.

There were no pads or substitutes in this Hamilton vs Toronto football game. The Canadian Football Association, formed in 1870, developed a unique version from soccer and rugby.

Toronto's Carleton track hosted the Hunt Club's grand steeplechases and just plain horseracing – with sidebets.

The game of lacrosse won converts across the border. A New York team played the Montreal Shamrocks, perhaps the best lacrosse team ever, for the American championship in 1874.

Royal Canadian Yacht Club members turned Lake Ontario's turbulent waters into a recreational sailors' paradise for sloops like the Coral, painted by Wm. Armstrong in 1873.

A formalized version of the barroom brawl, bare-knuckled boxing was the ultimate test of manhood.

Lacrosse on skates was great entertainment for the spectators; note the band behind them. But it soon gave way to ice hockey – the first organized game took place in Victoria Rink in 1875.

A CHALLENGE TO HANLAN.

To the Editor of the Sporting Times:

SIR,—I, the undersigned, do hereby challenge any man in the Dominion (Edward Hanlan preferred) to row a five mile sculling race on the Kennebecasis, in best and best boats, for the sum of one thousand dollars a side. Race to take place any time after Sept. 10th. I hereby deposit one hundred dollars as forfeit in the hands of the Editor of the SPORTING TIMES. This challenge to remain open until Sept. 1st.

WALLACE ROSS.

Hanlan, aged 22, wrested the Canadian championship title from Wallace Ross, a New Brunswicker, in 1877.

CHAPTER TWO

The Working Man and Uncle Sam

Nine hours a day, six days a week is enough for any man to work!

Workers' slogan in 1872 printers' strike.

Never had a parade, not even a royal parade so roused Toronto's passions as did this Monday march of the working men. The very thought of it split the city down the middle. The working class and labour press said it was a grand idea, the first real bid for liberty. The bosses considered it shameful, criminal, the beginnings of anarchy, and George Brown of the Toronto *Globe* urged free men to "stamp out" everything the parade stood for. On this April 15, 1872, Canadian workmen were actually going to demonstrate – to demand a shorter work week, from sixty to fifty-four hours. Next thing, the outraged employers told each other, these people would be wanting more *money*.

At noon the men formed up – two thousand of them, in rough ill-fitting woollen jackets, plug hats, heavy boots – outside the Trades Assembly Hall at 74 King Street West. People lined the boardwalks, leaned from windows and cheered as the marchers moved off. First came the British Ensign ("Off with your caps, there! God bless Her Majesty!"), followed by the scarlet and braid of the 10th Royal Grenadiers. Next, the iron moulders' union, the bricklayers' and masons' union and the unorganized workmen, marching four abreast.

Then the Band of Christian Brothers' Academy, blowing their hearts out on cornet and tuba. Next the unions of cigar makers, coopers, blacksmiths, machinists and bakers.

Behind them, *umpah, umpah,* came the Queen's Own Band; trudging behind it, the burnishers and polishers, the Knights of St. Crispin (a shoemakers' union), and the amalgamated engineers. Next the Young Irishmen's Band, followed by the Union Jack and Stars and Stripes entwined – a diplomatic touch. In Britain and the United States, the fifty-four-hour week was common and American unions offered their Canadian counterparts affiliation and support in the nine-hour movement.

Finally, the catalysts of the parade: the typographers' union. Two weeks before, the Toronto printers had struck for the nine-hour day and had been locked out. This march was in support of them. The procession took a square-shaped route through the main business section: Brock to Queen to George, then along King again and up to College Avenue. As it passed the office of the friendly Toronto *Leader* the men cheered; a few doors later, passing the *Globe*, they "maintained a contemptuous silence."

A spring snowflurry swirled around them but nobody cared. At Queen's Park, where marchers and crowd now numbered ten thousand, speakers mounted a platform to harangue the bosses. "Nine

The class system persisted even in the manufactory where bowler hats distinguished the master craftsmen from the ordinary factory hand.

Opposite page: Fire and brimstone were part of the working man's lot at the Toronto Rolling Mills, a scene painted by Wm. Armstrong.

**Daniel O'Donoghue
A Father of Canadian Labour**

To help support his widowed mother, O'Donoghue became a printer's apprentice in 1855 at the tender age of eleven. A later stint in the U.S. where American trade unions were suffering a few birth pangs, led to his involvement in Canada's nine-hour-day movement. Active in the formation of the CLU in 1873, the Ottawa printer initiated the practice of presenting the working man's views to government, and he became the first Independent labour member of the Ontario legislature.

Opposite page: Tradesmen under a dozen banners, including the Stars and Stripes, march through Hamilton streets bugling their plea for shorter hours, in June 1872.

hours a day, six days a week is enough for any man to work!" "Machines were invented by the working men. Are they not to receive some of the benefits arising therefrom?" "The wealth of this country is being increased by the energy of the working men of this country. We have no aristocracy here but the aristocracy of labour."

It seemed as though labour had won the day for sure, and the crowd went home in high spirits. Next day the bosses struck back: twenty-four of the striking printers were jailed for "criminal conspiracy in restraint of trade." But the law was repealed that year, and more strikes sprang up like bushfires from southern Ontario to the Maritimes.

For the 188,000 industrial labourers in the Dominion in 1870, life was, at best, mediocre. They were employed in making farm implements, beer, furniture, carriages, barrels, whisky, clothing, tools, flour, glass, railway cars, nails, rope, ships, soap, sewing machines, axles and sheet iron. They also worked in sugar and oil refineries, tanneries, print shops and foundries. Most companies were small and family owned, but even the kindest bosses saw little wrong with prevailing working conditions, which were all to their advantage.

annual wage: $185 - $245

The typical ten-hour day ran from 7:30 A.M. until 6:00 P.M. (The half-hour lunch break was on the employee's time.) There were no paid holidays, coffee breaks, pension plans or medical schemes. The average industrial worker's annual wage in 1870 ranged from $185 in Quebec to $245 in Ontario. But families needed the income and, with Canadian industry beginning to grow, even women and children flocked to the factories, despite the evil working conditions. Some places were mere converted houses, lacking proper heat or ventilation. Toilets, if indoors at all, had only a low partition separating men and women. Machinery

was driven by belts that tore off fingers, clothes and hair. Children of ten or eleven worked for as little as twenty-five cents a day. When machines ripped off their fingers, the employer scolded them for carelessness. In some factories, employees stood all day or suffered a five-cent fine per sit-down. There were also fines for theft, being late, or wasting material.

few qualified for franchise

Reform was long overdue. It was time, said the *Ontario Workman,* to "Organize! Organize! Organize!" Canadian labour had been organizing, after a fashion, for more than forty years. In 1827 Quebec printers formed a trade society. Tailors, shipwrights, bricklayers, miners, iron moulders, railroaders, coopers, carpenters and others followed suit. In 1871, fifteen trades' societies united as the Toronto Trades Assembly. When the criminal conspiracy law was repealed after the printers' strike, the Assembly invited other unions to join in the first national organization – the Canadian Labour Union, formed in 1873.

But the brute reality of the depression of the mid-seventies almost crushed this first attempt of labour to wield organized power. Even the worst job was better than none at all! Canadian workers felt singularly helpless in their plight. The CLU conventions pressed for political action and manhood suffrage, but, although Ontario in 1874 extended the franchise to men with annual incomes of $400 or more, few labourers qualified. A vote for all men over twenty-one was still years away, and women's franchise wouldn't come in the century. Thus the working class had little influence over the economic and political machinations of the seventies.

One problem that both the Tories and the Grits faced was to maintain Canadian manufacturers – and jobs – in the face of competition from

Santa Claus looks mournfully out on a world in the low years of the 1870s depression when the poor (right) suffer greater privation and only the wealthy (left) can afford to feast.

American firms who dumped cheaper products in Canada. With no power at the polls, the workers could only stand by and hope that their government would cope with the often militant and acquisitive Uncle Sam. For years he had jostled and tested Canada, jealously eyeing little pieces of it for himself. And Britain, at this point in history, was prepared to make enormous concessions to placate the Americans.

Brother Sam may show fight

The Treaty of Washington in 1871 provides a classic example of Yankee bullying and British waffling. American fishermen wanted free access to Canadian waters. Canada, having no reciprocal privileges, quite properly charged a licence fee, which the Americans ignored. Canadian and British ships seized some four hundred American lawbreakers in three months. Naturally Uncle Sam made angry noises and finally a British Commission, with John A. Macdonald as sole Canadian member, visited Washington to try to settle this and other grievances.

"I think this American fishery question bothers Sir John," wrote Lady Macdonald in her diary. "I suppose it is ticklish business as Brother Sam may show fight." Sir John *was* bothered. Britain would surely strive to pacify the Yanks at Canada's expense and Canadians would blame it all on him.

He was partly right. Between interminable Washington banquets that earned for the Joint High Commission the nickname "High Commission of Joints," Macdonald was wheedled, browbeaten and snubbed. His British colleagues treated him as a backwoods upstart. The Americans, at first, weren't sure who he was. And although John A. waged a long stubborn one-man fight, he was bound to lose. When the British found Macdonald wouldn't "reason" with them, they simply overruled him, broke their promise to Canada and sold the fishing rights for twelve years and $5,500,000.

On signing day the Americans decorated the room with spring flowers and offered a morning snack of strawberries and ice cream. John A. had no appetite. "Here go the fisheries," he murmured bitterly as he took up the pen. "We gave them away." Eventually he wrung from Britain a reward for having knuckled under at Washington: a loan that would help start the Canadian Pacific Railway.

Ironically, the railway soon brought Macdonald's downfall. In 1873 his government was swept away in the wake of the Pacific Scandal. Mackenzie's Grits came to power at the end of 1873 just as the world was sinking into depression. Prices fell, bankruptcies and unemployment soared and money markets tightened, making the raising of loans more difficult. Customs and excise duties, the major source of federal revenue, were hard hit. Although Mackenzie raised the duties slightly in 1874, the Grits, who were for free trade by philosophy, made no real move toward protection of the fledgling Canadian industries against American competition.

poking fun at America

But then, everything American had a profound effect on Canadian life. The long shadow of Uncle Sam was everywhere. His craggy face with little goatee and stovepipe hat peered out from a thousand newspaper cartoons. His policies, manners, gadgets and meddling touched the lives of all Canadians.

Indeed, Uncle Sam was so omnipresent and sometimes menacing that poking fun at America became something of a Canadian national pastime. Children's books featured as their bad guy a "Yankee storekeeper" with cunning eyes and unshaven jaw or "a sallow State's man bolting his breakfast with unconscionable speed and between

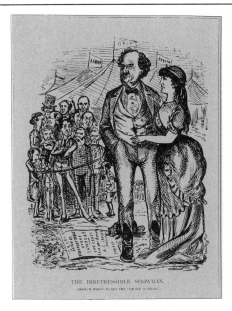

THE IRREPRESSIBLE SHOWMAN.
BARNUM WANTS TO BUY THE "PACIFIC SCANDAL."

The Parliamentary Circus, 1873

P.T. Barnum's summer tour (left) inspired Canada's greatest cartoonist, J.W. Bengough of *Grip,* to capture the main acrobats in the Pacific Scandal drama (below). Accusations and revelations ("I must have another ten thousand") were followed by passionate denials ("These hands are clean"). As the fateful fall session of parliament was about to open, the question "Will he get through?" remained for Sir John A., the bareback rider, who had successfully passed through the easy hoop, held by Governor General Dufferin. "The prophecy conveyed in the unreasonable smallness of the hoop in the clown's [Mackenzie's] hand was duly realized." George Brown looks on as circus ringmaster.

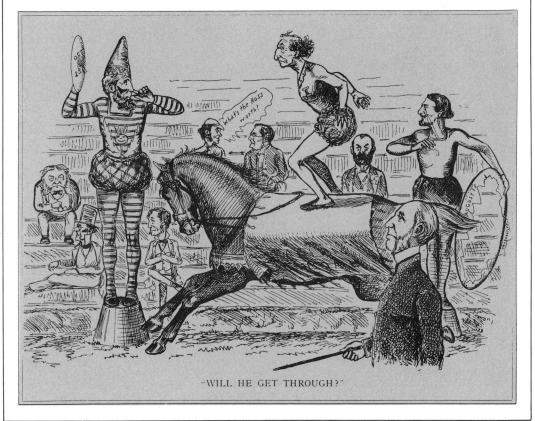

"WILL HE GET THROUGH?"

**Edward Blake
Voice of the Grits**

A brilliant lawyer and a restless politician, Edward Blake was thirty-eight when he became Liberal premier of Ontario in 1871. He resigned a year later and turned his political and oratorical powers to opposing John A. Macdonald in Ottawa. The towering, neurotic Blake became a major voice in the Canada First movement, dismaying old-line Liberals by his erratic behavior. Although leader of the Liberal party in the 1880s, he never realized his ambition to become the prime minister of Canada.

times in a high treble voice volunteering his opinions upon all Canadian matters as if he were endowed with a special commission to set them right."

For all their fears and carping, Canadians secretly envied and admired Uncle Sam. They sang American songs and read American novels (*Uncle Tom's Cabin* was still the great favourite). American romantic serials ran endlessly in Canadian newspapers. So did American news which invariably had the juiciest crimes and sex scandals. Minstrel shows, drama companies, circuses – and labour unions – all brought their charms and talents over the line.

Yankee notions

American cities awed the little nation to the north. There was New York, brawling, towering, sprawling, with 942,000 people in 1870, more than Manitoba, British Columbia and the Maritimes combined. There was Chicago, twice the size of Montreal, a full-grown muscular city with heavy horses dragging great drays of bulky freight through its busy streets and whole fleets of steamers lying packed against its crowded quay. When Chicago burned in 1871, Canadians, who also lived with the daily terror of fire, mourned as though it were their own.

And Canadians by the score journeyed to Philadelphia for the Centennial Exhibition of 1876. "It would be very strange to find anyone who owed a bill paying it just now rather than go to Philadelphia," sniffed the *Monetary Times*. And why not? The exhibition was showing off America's greatest talent: invention and manufacturing. Despite the competition this talent provided, Canadians were fascinated by "Yankee notions," the name for any kind of gadgetry – a can opener, a rotary bread cutter, a patent fly trap, an egg beater, potato peeler, friction match box,

weather vane, sewing machine, washing machine – and naturally wanted to obtain such clever products of American ingenuity.

By the seventies, industry was a simple fact of life in America. Everything about it was larger than life, too. Its Pennsylvania oil fields were richer and rowdier than anything around little Oil Springs, Ontario. American canneries turned out thirty million tins of food a year. Its grain terminals were immense; its factories with their assembly lines were the marvel of the age; its railways leaped across a continent. And its workers made more money. They also paid higher prices but still they lived better than Canadians. In 1874 an American tailor could earn up to $3.00 a day; the Canadian's top wage was $2.50. In most other trades, the American earned fifty cents to a dollar a day more. American workers usually received an annual holiday, too, which was virtually unknown in Canada.

With such attractions, there began a steady exodus of Canadian workers to the south. America, despite its own depression pains, offered a man more opportunity. By the end of the decade Maritimes fishermen, Quebec lumbermen, Ontario farmers, railwaymen, industrial workers and professional men by the thousands had streamed across the border.

milk at 7 cents a quart

For those who stuck it out in Canada, life was bleak. A thrifty family could just eke out an existence. An 1873 study of a Hamilton worker with wife and five children showed weekly expenses of $13.81. With that he could buy roasting beef or veal cutlets at 10 cents a pound, butter at 25 cents a pound, milk at 7 cents a quart, eggs at 25 cents a dozen, potatoes at 60 cents a bushel and bread made from flour at $7 a barrel. It also paid for lamp-oil, fuel (a big item: coal and wood were

$8 per ton and per cord, respectively) and above-average rent of $13.50 a month. It allowed nothing for liquor, tobacco or luxuries. The family took no holidays. With $100 for the year's clothing and $24 for taxes, the annual expenditures totalled $842.36. So, although relatively well-paid at $15 a week, this worker came out $62.36 in the red.

the accessible tavern

Most other families in that particular study broke even or actually saved a few dollars in a year. But for what? At prices of $2,500 to $4,000 and with interest rates of ten percent, a house was out of the question, so they rented quarters in a tenement with several other families. Rent for a four-room place (kitchen plus three other rooms to use as they chose) averaged $3 to $8 a month; six rooms averaged $12 a month. A tenement was the poorest form of habitation: cold in winter, stifling in summer, with an outdoor privy shared by several other families. There were no bathing facilities, at home or anywhere.

"Criminals are usually surrounded at public expense by the best or at least most improved sanitary conditions," observed Toronto's *Sanitary Journal* in 1879. "The poor labouring man is permitted to live on in want and unhealthy surroundings, frequently without the means or knowledge to obtain the essentials of health and life."

When the labourer got home after work, he had little energy or daylight for outdoor sports. Newspapers, even at three cents a day, were a luxury; anyway, he was probably one of the 300,000 Canadian adults who couldn't read. His tastes and budget didn't run to a fifty-cent seat at the theatre.

That left the tavern, a cheap and accessible way of forgetting one's troubles. Whisky was only thirty or forty cents a gallon and Toronto, as an example, had a tavern for every seventy adults.

Canada First

The first outburst of Canadian nationalism, the Canada First movement originated at the height of enthusiasm for Confederation. An appropriate symbol, "Young Canada," (left) first appeared in 1869 in the magazine, *Grinchuckle.* In the seventies, he grew into Johnny Canuck, ever more heroic and handsome, the image of a nation daring to stand on its feet. With the arrival of Goldwin Smith (below) in 1872 and the active participation of Edward Blake, the years 1874-75 saw the height of the movement's influence. But like its publications, the *Nation* and the *Liberal,* Canada First did not survive. Goldwin Smith's talents and money kept their literary journal *Canadian Monthly and National Review* alive longer, although he himself later turned away from nationalist sentiment to advocate union with the U.S.

WITH THE COMPLIMENTS of
"CANADA'S·GREATEST·MUSIC·HOUSE"

CANADA FIRST

MARCH·TWO·STEP

FOR

PIANO

WHALEY ROYCE & CO. LIMITED.
356 MAIN STREET
WINNIPEG MAN.
PHONE. 263

Price 50¢

·EVERYTHING·IN·MUSIC·

Stalwarts of Mr. Gurd's lacrosse team beneath the Montreal company's banner frame unsmiling co-workers and family members at the annual picnic.

Tavern-keepers didn't care about a man's dress or social standing. Indeed, at Joe Beef's Canteen in Montreal, the thick-necked Irish proprietor catered especially to workmen and down-and-outers. ("Joe is every man's countryman," he advertised. "He will take five cents from a rank Orangeman as well as a live Fenian.")

In both cities, drunks accounted for more than half the arrests. Drunkenness was such a national problem that two durable institutions arose to haunt generations of Canadian tipplers: the Canada Temperance Act (providing a simplified form of local option across the country) and the Woman's Christian Temperance Union.

Working people as a group were the heaviest drinkers. But as the *Nation* pointed out, in 1875, it was "not so much a vice as an uncontrollable disease, the result of overwork in heated factories, nervous depression arising from the bad air of ill-ventilated and ill-drained dwellings or even total want of cheerful recreation."

the company picnic

The recreational highlight of a worker's year was the trades or company picnic. Let us look in briefly on the fourth annual picnic of the Toronto plumbers, brass finishers and steamfitters. It is Saturday, August 31, 1872. West Lodge Gardens, a pleasant green park, is alive with screaming children on swings, women in their best gingham gingerly tapping croquet balls, men shedding their frock-coats and loosening uncomfortable collars for a game of baseball. A few employers are moving benevolently through the throng, accepting handshakes and tipping their hats. *Decent of them to turn out!*

And now the events we have all been waiting for: the quoit throw, standing high jump, hammer throw, augur shoot, standing long leap, three quick jumps, velocipede slow race, apprentices's race. . . .

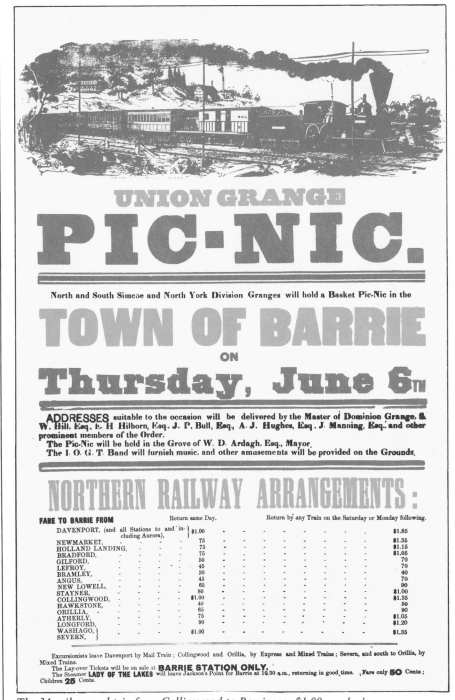

The 34-mile round trip from Collingwood to Barrie was $1.00 – a day's wage.

There goes John Coulson, winning the 100-yard-race and a silver cake basket! And would you look at old John Fogg – won the sack race and got himself a real silk hat! Good prizes this year: silver butter cooler, pocket-watch stand, silver tobacco box, set of cutlery, silver cruet stand. Good food, too: pounds of ham, roast beef, chicken, pie, cake, ice cream; gallons of lemonade and beer. Near evening, there is dancing to Lubar's Quadrille Band. But all too soon, back aboard the horse-cars and home again to the stuffy tenements.

A Saturday like this merely pointed up the drudgery of all the others. Some enlightened thinkers began to argue that a shorter work week might even be good for employers too, by increasing productivity. Why shouldn't workers have time for walks in the woods, the fellowship of other mortals, the improvement of physical and mental health? "Who can tell," prodded the *Sanitary Journal* in 1874, "that they would not thereby be rendered more happy, healthful and useful?"

But the nine-hour movement made painfully slow progress, and the first ills of unionism began to show up: sloppy workmanship, irresponsible action during strikes, and bullying of non-conformist workers. During a Grand Trunk Railway strike in 1877, the engineers at the appointed hour abandoned trains and passengers on the spot even in snowstorms miles from any town. The *Monetary Times* reported that "it is almost impossible to get really good work done in almost every department of labour. The tendency of all trade associations is to put the inefficient man on the same level as the efficient. There is no stimulus to good work." And labourers who dared to buck the unions became known as "scabs" or "rats."

If the labour movement was still floundering, the country at least was clambering back to its feet. Macdonald swept back into office in 1878, capitalizing on the failure of Mackenzie's free trade stand with his National Policy that proposed protective tariffs for Canadian manufacturers and promised employment above all. At first it seemed to work because the depression was ending: business failures decreased; production and exports increased. But the National Policy was no economic panacea. Many other factors contributed to Canada's recovery, including America's own emergence from the depression. In fact, some of the first manufacturers to take advantage of the new tariffs were Americans who set up branch plants across the border. Like it or not, Canadians realized that their economic pulse beat to the same tempo as Uncle Sam's.

THE POLICY "GIVEN AWAY!"

Grip expected the Policy to be a great embarrassment.

John A's Triumphant Return

Defying all predictions, Sir John A. did not fade away after the drubbing of Pacific Scandal days. In one sense, the depression was his ally; as Mackenzie's Grits struggled with its effects on the economy, Macdonald began to solidify his influence with the electorate through a series of summer political picnics from 1876 to the election in 1878. Taking a calculated risk in adopting a "national policy" of tariff protection, he was forgiven his sins by the voters who then kept him in power until his death in 1891.

VICTORIA HARBOR

VICTORIA HARBOR

JAMES BAY

STRAITS OF

CHAPTER THREE

A Rare and Glorious Human Brew

I would not object to a little revolution... if after Confederation we were treated unfairly.

Amor de Cosmos, Premier of B.C., 1872-74

The first of many mystified Easterners to attempt to define British Columbia's extraordinary personality was an emissary from the federal government named J.D. Edgar. In June 1874, after spending some time among the gold miners, toffs, Yank-lovers, Yank-haters, hurdy-gurdy girls, lumberjacks, Chinese houseboys, little old English ladies and outright kooks who had recently condescended to join the Dominion, the bemused Edgar reported to his Secretary of State: "A population of peculiar intelligence!"

That was the understatement of the year. The whole story of British Columbia was its characters. They were indeed intelligent as well as crafty, crotchety, uninhibited, independent and totally unpredictable. They brought to Confederation a rare and glorious human brew that the Fathers and other Canadians never quite understood.

A stranger, on viewing Victoria's winding lanes and prim gardens, its cricket games on Beacon Hill, and advertisements for seven-octave pianos and crystal goblets, was convinced he'd found the only civilized spot west of Hampton Court. A couple of nights later, cowering in a Gastown saloon while two Cariboo miners beat each other up with chairs, he knew he'd made an awful mistake. Then on reading in the Cariboo *Sentinel* that for twelve dollars a month payable in advance, miners could take "instruction in Arithmetic, French, Spanish, English grammar, English composition and the dead languages," he guessed that British Columbia was cultured after all. Except, there in Gastown was Black's *abattoir,* where sheep and cattle were slaughtered on an open platform in full view of the public.

The visitor reeled from paradox to paradox: New Westminster's annual May Day festival with May queen and dances round the maypole; murders; the Hyack fire department annual picnic at which "gladsome couples whirled in mazy gracefulness" and "amusements were improvised for the little people who frisked in gladsome frolic to the music of their own sweet voices"; opium dens; a raffle of stuffed birds, "the most beautiful array of the feathered denizens of our forests." No use trying to understand British Columbians. Was it the sea air? Or the fact that mountains sealed them off from the rest of Canada? Was it the sheer beneficence of nature?

Certainly, few coastal and Vancouver Island people had ever really pioneered, ever known the sheer animal struggle between man and elements that leaves no time for high-minded thought. But the British Columbia interior was rugged enough; you had only to ride a stage down the Cariboo

Here stands Gassy Jack Deighton in a sober pose. One of the first citizens of Granville (Vancouver), he could usually be found behind the bar in his Gastown Hotel.

Opposite page: This 1878 bird's-eye view of Victoria, looking north on the harbour and principal streets, justifies its description as "the only civilized spot" in the West.

37

Trail to appreciate that. British Columbians even drove their coaches with flair. They whipped the four-horse vehicles along those twisting rock-strewn trails, sheer cliff above, five-hundred-foot drop below, with never a "Whoa" or touch of foot brake. Mule trains pulled to the very brink of a precipice to yield the right of way, and the stage thundered on to the next station where fresh horses with polished hooves and harness waited. At night you slept on a bench in a rude wayside hotel and rose to a breakfast of ham, eggs and a durable kind of flapjack known as "Rocky Mountain deadshot."

But mostly British Columbia dropped its largesse right into people's laps. The ocean wriggled with cod, herring, halibut, haddock and oysters. Fat red salmon at ten cents were so common the canneries used only the bellies. Sockeye salmon were sold for fertilizer. For a long time no one bothered to catch the five-hundred-pound sturgeon since British Columbians didn't fancy the white meat. Finally sturgeon began to sell for one and a half cents a pound.

no hunting licence required

A homesteader, after getting a hundred and sixty free acres from the government, grew plump pears, pumpkins two and a half feet high, and juicy apples, six inches in diameter. The forests were choked with game, and no hunting licence was required. But it was hardly worth buying ammunition when venison hams sold in stores for six cents a pound and grouse at fifty cents a brace. Wages in British Columbia were high by Canadian standards: blacksmiths made $4.00 a day; mechanics and plumbers, $3.50; cooks, $35.00 a month and board. And the climate, as the provincial agent-general in London assured prospective immigrants, was of a salubrity enjoyed nowhere else in the world.

So, a newcomer could relax and indulge in the luxury of using his wits. "Gassy Jack" Deighton did just that. A great barrel of a man with purple complexion and a silver tongue that was never still, he had floated a canoe into Burrard Inlet one rainy autumn afternoon in 1867 with an Indian wife, a yellow dog, two chickens and a keg of whisky. He opened the keg and announced he was a poor but honest man who needed volunteers to help build a saloon. In twenty-four hours the place was up and the whisky gone. (For a time, the cluster around his saloon was dubbed Gastown.) Gassy Jack climbed up on the roof, unfurled a Union Jack and made an emotional little speech in support of England.

patriots and Yankee-lovers

That was another thing about British Columbia – it was either violently for or violently against Britain. There were patriots like miner Johnny Bryant of the Omineca gold fields, who flew a Union Jack of blue overalls, white flour sacks and red underwear. Victoria was packed with men who, said Governor General Dufferin, "had the middle class Englishman's vulgar contempt for everything that is not English."

Yet other residents celebrated Washington's birthday with military salutes, greeted the Fourth of July with fireworks and hung pictures of Lincoln and Grant in their saloons. America wanted British Columbia as a corridor to the recently acquired territory of Alaska. Geographically, the British colony was much closer to the United States. Yet John A. Macdonald was just as determined to anchor his sprawling loose-knit nation.

What gifts could a suitor offer a place so heaven-blessed as British Columbia? The Americans offered American citizenship which, they judged, was enough to bring any heathen people

A Coastful of Characters

The gold rushes of the 1850s and 1860s had gathered to British Columbia from the ends of the earth a wide assortment of lone adventurers and groups of earnest immigrants who stayed on to shape the province that entered Confederation in 1871.

Matthew Baillie Begbie (left), six-foot-five, roamed B.C. dispensing a stern brand of justice. Often called inaccurately "the hanging judge," Begbie was knighted in 1875.

By 1875, B.C.'s legislators had worked themselves into a furor over delays in the promised railroad. The man in profile in front of the door is Premier George Walkem.

Surveyor, geologist and botanist George Dawson (third from left) and party in 1879 at Fort McLeod, B.C. Eventually he gave his name to Dawson City in the Yukon.

British sailors lounge by beached canoes in front of Nootka Indian houses in 1873 (above). John Robson (right), editor, legislator, CPR paymaster and future provincial premier.

Amor de Cosmos
"Lover of the Universe"

Nova-Scotia-born William Smith
followed the lure of gold from
California, (where he changed his
name to Amor de Cosmos) to B.C.
In the pages of his newspaper, the
Victoria *Colonist,* he advocated
the union of the colonies of B.C.
and Vancouver Island. An active
and ambitious politician, he won
a seat in the House of Commons and
then held the premiership of the
province from 1872 to 1874.

gratefully to its knees. John A. offered a railroad, to be started within two years and completed in ten – an outrageous gamble and a goody that even the startled British Columbians didn't expect.

Nevertheless, they debated it long in their legislature – a typically rakish set of pagoda-shaped red buildings called the "Bird Cages." Those in favour of annexation to the States fought hard. After all, America already *had* a transcontinental railway, which could be linked to British Columbia. Macdonald's west coast ally – a bearded prophet with burning eyes, who had changed his name from William Smith to Amor de Cosmos (Lover of the Universe) – vehemently argued Confederation's cause. Yet Macdonald must have flinched on learning that, during debate, de Cosmos said, "I would not object to a little revolution now and again if, after Confederation, we were treated unfairly." However this was just talk to remind the East that British Columbia was not to be taken for granted. In July 1871, the new province came in and "people met on the streets and shook hands with and congratulated each other, and cheered and cheered and cheered."

rollicking along as usual

Off to the Dominion Parliament went the first representatives and their wives. Being British Columbians, they were critical and sometimes tactless. Ottawa, observed one wife, "all seems so flat." Few of its shops were as nice as the London House in Victoria, sniffed another. "I never in my life saw such a collection of downright *ugly* and awkward looking men," declared a third. A new senator for British Columbia proclaimed flatly, "All Ottawa men are intensely stupid." One new M.P. attended an elegant party with a brandy bottle peeping from his pocket.

Meanwhile, back across the Rockies, things were rollicking along as usual. Gassy Jack was

getting wealthy on booze. A good roast beef dinner with soup and dessert could be had for twenty-five cents in New Westminster. A gold rush was on 250 miles north of Quesnel, and in 1874, its peak year, miners took a million dollars in ore from this Cassiar region. The strike wasn't much by British Columbia standards but the supporting cast was. "Dancing Bill" Latham and his dusky Indian maidens entertained the boys. Good-hearted Nellie Cashman started a profitable hotel in the mining town of Laketon, went out for a holiday, heard some of "her boys" were dying of scurvy, hurried back with life-saving medicine and was known ever after as "the angel of the Cassiar."

"Don't prevaricate, sir!"

Laketon also pointed with pride to Sam Sing, miner and devil-fighter. Sam, when drunk, was pestered by devils visible only to him. Finally in the interests of self-defence he got a pistol. That night, Sam stepped into the street and, while startled residents hit the dirt, gunned down all the devils he could see and sank into an alcoholic coma. His friends believed him dead, prepared a magnificent funeral feast and bought a twenty-five dollar coffin. Just as the lid was going down, Sam rose up with a puzzled expression. His friends took to the woods, screaming. Sam polished off the feast, gathered his devils and vanished forever.

Drinkers, gamblers, philosophers, wits – the miners were admirably suited to British Columbia. "Don't prevaricate, sir!" thundered a judge to a witness in a gold fields court case. "Can't help it, judge," the miner answered. "Ever since I got a kick in the mouth from a mule that knocked my teeth out, I prevaricate a good deal."

That judge must have been the incomparable Matthew Baillie Begbie. Six-foot-five, handsome, Cambridge-educated and son of a Scottish army colonel, Begbie roamed the gold country for nearly thirty years, doling out a peculiar justice that was probably right for the time. He travelled with a dozen horses and held court in cabins, barns or from his saddle. On minor cases, he was prosecutor, defence and judge. Serious crimes required a jury, but Begbie expected jurymen to conform to his preconceived ideas. When one murder suspect was found guilty only of manslaughter, Begbie shrilled, "You deserve to be hanged! If the jury had performed their duty I would have had the painful satisfaction of condemning you to death!" Then he turned on the jury. "And you, gentlemen, are a pack of Dallas horse thieves. I can say it would give me great pleasure to see you hanged, each and every one of you."

Naturally Begbie had many enemies. The Cariboo people once sent a deputation to Victoria to have him removed. He frequently had to fight in self-defence, but he never backed down. Once, lounging on the second-floor balcony of his hotel, he heard some toughs below plotting his assassination. The judge dumped a chamber pot on their heads and went back to his rest.

For all his bluster he was generally fair. He was one of a very few white men to stand up for the Chinese, whose relentless persecution began in the seventies and went on for generations. At a later royal commission investigation of the allegedly harmful wave of immigration, Begbie declared the Chinese were not, as charged, more criminal or immoral than white men. He went on to say:

Their religion, notions of honour and rank, mode of thought, dress, amusements, sense of beauty are not to our taste. Their language appears to us ridiculous. Yet they as evidently despise all our attainments and ways and they come here and beat us on our own ground in supplying our own

New Westminster's May Day Queen and attendants cluster around the maypole wearing the fashionable bonnets of '71.

**Lord Dufferin
Governor General, 1872-1878**

Frederick Temple Blackwood, the Earl of Dufferin, an eloquent, witty and popular diplomat, was appointed governor general of Canada in 1872. The Dufferins travelled coast to coast by vice-regal railway coach, but the only transcontinental route was through the United States! In 1876, placating British Columbians upset by the delay in railroad construction, he ended a masterly speech with the words: "and if ever I have the good fortune to come to British Columbia again, I hope it may be — by rail."

wants. They are inferior in weight and size of muscle and yet they work more steadily and with better success on the average than white men.

The Chinese also worked for less money, and this was why they were scorned. They'd come to Canada for gold, usually working the meagre claims abandoned by white men. When the gold rush petered out they turned to storekeeping, trading, farming, gardening and domestic service. They were patient, industrious men in pigtails who had usually left their families behind and were bitterly lonely. They clanned together in crowded quarters and smoked a little opium, as at home. They wanted to be good citizens. When the Dufferins visited British Columbia in 1876 the Chinese community held open house for all the whites, offering tea and sweetmeats.

persecution of the Chinese

But the whites spurned them and the abuse increased. Amor de Cosmos was one of the main anti-Chinese agitators, and it may have given them comfort to see him run into a hornet's nest of his own. He was premier from 1872-74, a bad time to hold the job. The CPR was still nowhere near its promised start and British Columbians, never noted for their patience, were becoming downright cranky.

Macdonald's government had fallen in the Pacific Scandal of the previous year when it was proven his Tories had received at least $350,000 in campaign funds from the men who'd been awarded the railway contracts. To new Prime Minister Alexander Mackenzie, a dry unimaginative stonemason, the CPR was the Tories' bastard child, unwanted on his doorstep. It looked like Canada was welshing on its promise. What was Premier de Cosmos doing about it? One day eight hundred angry citizens marched into the Bird Cages chanting, "We'll hang de Cosmos on a sour apple tree." The Lover of the Universe hid out in the Speaker's room.

"Speed the railway"

When that demonstration produced no results the British Columbians aimed lengthy petitions and pointed hints at the visiting governor general. The parade-route arches cried "Speed the Railway," "Good But Not Iron" (a live horse stood by the arch) and "Our Railroad or Separation" (Dufferin refused to drive under that one). Still no action, so British Columbia took its plea right to the top – to Queen Victoria. When that failed, the province announced in 1878 it would leave Confederation if the railway wasn't finished in two years.

But by then John A. was back in power with a strong majority. He was even a West Coast M.P. In winning the country, he'd lost his Kingston seat and had to take a by-election in Victoria. He pushed the railway plans through. Four months after the decade ended, a dynamite blast at Yale signaled the beginning of the long-awaited CPR and British Columbia stayed in Confederation.

A Lady's Journal

The charming Lady Dufferin, whose *Canadian Journal* offers delightful accounts of vice-regal pleasures and misadventures, left many visual impressions of Canadian scenery and of the life style of the decade. On their 1876 visit to B.C., the Dufferins explored the Indian mission village of Metlakatla and Skidegate on the Queen Charlotte Islands. The captions for her water-colour sketches are her own impressions as recorded in her journal.

"Metlacatlah is one of the most successful of Indian missions. . . . The Church . . . is quite new, having been built entirely by Mr. Duncan [the missionary] and the Indians. . . . Of course it is made of wood, and is perfectly simple; but the proportions and the simplicity together give quite a grand effect."

Lady Dufferin sketched by her husband.

"We had a splendid passage over to Queen Charlotte's Islands. I suppose this is the wildest place I shall ever be at. We anchored opposite a village, which, in the distance, looked like a forest of bare poles. Every house seems to have one; they are highly valued, as symbols of rank."

By the end of the decade, Assiniboine and Ojibway, Cree and Blackfoot had formally ceded title to the vast lands of the North-West. Artist Sydney Hall of the London Graphic painted this scene of the Blackfoot swearing allegiance to the governor general, Lord Lorne, son-in-law of Queen Victoria, on his 1881 tour of Canada.

CHAPTER FOUR

From Tail Creek Town to Fort Carlton

It is a crying shame that the half-breeds have been ignored. It will result in trouble. . . .

Lieutenant-Governor Morris to Hector Langevin, 1878

For the tough, swarthy people of Tail Creek Town, the hunt was everything. The prairie was still dark with buffalo, early in the decade. Old men said the herds were smaller now, but there seemed to be no end to them. By the thousands they moved wherever good grass could be found, even braving the vicious winters as long as they could paw through shallow snow to that delicious "prairie wool," drifting into the United States sometimes but with no regular migratory pattern. For the Métis of Tail Creek Town, in the land someday to be called Alberta, the buffalo were food, clothing, spending money, fuel, harness, tents, rope and thread. Between hunts some Métis farmed, after a fashion, in tiny neighbouring communities with names that rang like church bells: St. Albert, Lac Ste. Anne, Lac la Biche. But life revolved around the shaggy buffalo.

It was the same all over the western plains in the seventies. Business, pleasure, tragedy, history could all be traced to the buffalo. American traders moved freely into the land no longer governed by the powerful Hudson's Bay Company, traded rotgut whisky for the Indians' buffalo skins, incited a massacre in the Cypress Hills and caused

an uneasy Macdonald government to establish the North-West Mounted Police. As the decade began, new ways of life, pressing in on the old nomadic ones, had sparked a Métis rebellion.

Part-white and part-Indian yet not totally comfortable in either world, the Métis were a hybrid race in search of a permanent home. Manitoba had been home once, but there the old life – hunting, trapping and farming small rectangular tracts running Quebec-style to the banks of the Red River – was vanishing under the onrush of settlement. Canada had bought Rupert's Land and the North-West Territories from the Hudson's Bay Company in 1869, without consulting the Red River settlers. Even before the official takeover, federal land surveyors were tramping over Métis farms.

Some, like young Louis Riel – well-educated, an orator, a natural leader but with resentment smouldering in his dark eyes – tried to forestall the inevitable. In November 1869, Riel and his men took Fort Garry in a bloodless coup, organized a provisional government with equal English-Métis representation and drafted a Bill of Rights seeking responsible provincial government, Métis ownership of their own land and fair representation in Parliament. Then Riel's foolhardy execution of Thomas Scott, a troublemaker who also happened to be an Ontario Orangeman, set off a torrent of racial, religious and political passion. Riel fled into

J.F. Macleod's C.M.G. medal.

Dress pouch and shoulder belt of Sgt-Major Steele.

Sabretache pouch of Major Walsh.

Adams Model 1872, six shot revolver.

Regimentally marked china, used by the Force.

Constable's dress tunic, 1876 pattern.

*Japanned (lacquered) metal container
for carrying white cork helmet.*

*Field glasses case emblazoned with motto.
Note the belt loops for easy carrying.*

Outfitting the N.W.M.P.

The scarlet tunics and white helmets of the Mounted Police became the symbol of authority on the prairies after the Force's organization in 1873. The first uniforms consisted of the scarlet Norfolk jacket, steel-grey or flesh-coloured breeches, blue trousers with a double white stripe, black or brown boots and pill-box hat or white cork helmet, as seen below.

James Farquharson Macleod, assistant commissioner in 1874, commissioner in 1877, founder of Fort Macleod.

temporary exile. The Wolseley military expedition came from the East, adding to the bitterness.

Other Métis had fled Manitoba years before in search of their own kind of life. For a while they'd found it around Tail Creek Town, east of what is now Red Deer. In the late sixties, their wandering hunting parties had taken shelter among 200-foot cutbanks and steep ravines choked with poplar and spruce. Now from early autumn until late spring it was home for as many as a thousand people.

It was a town without streets, simply a random scattering of four-hundred one-room log or sod shacks with packed-earth floors. Slab doors swung from buffalo-hide hinges. Light filtered anaemically through the tanned buffalo-calf-hide window panes, on to rough-hewn pole bunks, log stools and split-log tables. Dried buffalo chips smouldered on hearths of local sandstone, sometimes with stone chimneys but more often with flues of dried sod bricks. Yet for a few years this primitive town *was* the West, the biggest community between St. Boniface and the Pacific.

the hunting party

A hunt might happen any time when food ran low, but most often it was after the first spring thaw or first autumn frost. Then three to four hundred people with horses, carts, and dogs moved out of Tail Creek Town. The men were a hard-eyed, shaggy-moustached lot in moccasins, fringed buckskins and slouch hats, and they were total professionals.

Though carefree by nature, the Métis ran every hunt by strictest rule and ritual. Far ahead rode the scouts, wise and watchful loners who knew each wrinkle of the prairie by heart. They also knew how to kill a hostile Indian scout, instantly and noiselessly, when necessary; read a trail from a few broken twigs or a dent in the grass; distinguish the scent of buffalo from the multitude of odours

No visiting theatrical companies for Winnipeg; its citizens and the militia stationed there put on their own entertainment at the Theatre Royal.

49

Boundary Commission photographers took this portrait of Trader McPherson's family, Scots Métis of the Selkirk Settlement, near Lake of the Woods in 1873.

that rode the everlasting wind; slip animal-like to the very edge of a herd without spooking it.

Behind them, noisy but orderly, each hunter drove a Red River cart and led one or two fast saddle horses. Often the women and maybe the older children followed with other carts, anticipating a good haul of the huge carcasses. At every turn of the wheels the carts, held together by wooden pegs and rawhide strips, groaned and screeched like doomed souls. Dogs yapped. Horses snuffled. Drivers sang. It was a happy time for these proud people.

As the hunting party creaked along, a makeshift flag flew from the lead cart, marking the captain of the day. For that day, his word was law; he led the march, chose the night camp and directed the shaping of carts in a circle, hub to hub with shafts inward. Here the horses were corralled overnight and bedrolls or tipis set up. Outside this barrier men lit fires and posted sentries. Then the camp crier circled the enclosure calling "Oh ho, oh ho, le conseil!" And the Métis democratically chose captain and lieutenants for the next day.

rippling mass of buffalo

There came a day when the far-ranging scouts spotted a rippling dark brown mass of buffalo. That night the captain reviewed the rules. Theft would not be tolerated, neither would individualism since one impulsive solo run could stampede a herd and ruin the entire hunt. The penalties were harshly tailored to the occasion: for a first violation, the offender's saddle was cut to pieces; for the second, his coat was torn off; for the third, he was flogged.

At daybreak the hunters checked their Winchesters, Henrys or flint-locks, saddled up and quietly rode out. They closed in silently against the wind so the buffalo would not catch their scent. At the last point of shelter, generally a hill, they formed a line. Sometimes an older man hastily murmured a prayer, the others responding. Then all eyes turned to the captain's up-raised arm. It dropped! The hunt was on!

As the riders cleared the hill, the buffalo raised their massive low-slung heads, whirled with astonishing speed and were off like a thousand freight trains, cows and calves in front, protective bulls in the rear. Into this seething mass charged the hunters, firing from the saddle at point-blank range, aiming for the plump tender cows, reloading at the gallop, directing their horses with the knees.

buffalo tongue a delicacy

Some white men hunted from ambush, which was safer and good enough if you only wanted one robe and a few meals. Many Indians ran the herds over cliffs or into corrals. But the galloping close-up shot was a sure way, and least damaging to the hides which were important to these professionals. It was exceedingly dangerous. One misstep into a gopher or badger hole, one charge from a pain-crazed bull, and the fallen rider was gored or trampled to death. But this was the swashbuckling way in which great hunters were recognized. Two or three runs per man was the average; by then the land was littered with carcasses. But the all-time champion of Tail Creek was Abraham Salois — 600 kills in a single season, 37 in one run.

Afterward, still keyed up by the exhilaration of the kill, the Métis swiftly set about butchering, Indian-style: quick slashes to remove the feet and peel back the hide, a clean cut along the backbone leaving the sinew intact, more quick chops to sever the ribs. Into the carts went hides, tenderloins, humps, and the delicacies, liver and tongue.

Singing, shouting, joking, they drove back to their town, in and around the *Y* where Tail Creek meets the Red Deer River. Then the women's work began. They unloaded the carts, kicking the dogs

away, and cut the meat into smaller portions. In winter they froze and cached the chunks for future use. In summer they cut choice pieces into long strips and dried them on frames near a smoky fire that kept away the flies. Many delicious tongues were set aside for Tail Creek feasts; others were salted and sold to traders, who painted them with molasses for the gourmet markets in the East.

Before the work was done, Tail Creek Town threw the post-hunt party. First a feast of buffalo tongues and roasts, prairie chicken, wild duck eggs, flapjacks, bannock and roast beaver. Then some of the men withdrew for interminable smoke-clouded poker games. For most other Métis, dancing was the abiding passion. They danced often, hard and anywhere. On long trips some carried an old door in their carts so that at night, around the fire to fiddle or accordion, they could rat-a-tat-tat through a jig or reel.

the Mounties arrive

They were dancing when the Mounties arrived on their first recorded visit to Tail Creek Town in January 1875. By then, although the Police had been on the job less than four months, they had cut the whisky traffic to a trickle. But the grapevine had reported that a few diehard traders were heading for Tail Creek Town to see if they could swap a few gallons of rotgut for furs or horses. Inspector W.D. Jarvis, Sergeant-Major Sam Steele and twelve men rode down from Fort Edmonton to discourage them.

It was a hundred-mile trip through the worst cold spell in thirty years — 42 to 56 degrees below zero every day. The Mounties had no tents or stoves. For most of them it was the first prairie winter, a kind the folks back home just wouldn't have believed. Fortunately there were Métis scouts and a few hardened Army veterans to teach the ex-bank clerks and farm boys in the Force the

Jerry Potts, a Métis who acted as guide and interpreter for the N.W.M.P. on their trek westward in 1874 to put a stop to whisky trading around Fort Whoop-Up.

Ambroise Lépine
The Man Who Shot Tom Scott

Riel's second-in-command, Ambroise Lépine organized the court martial and execution of Thomas Scott in March 1870. Ontario's bitter feeling of resentment led to Lépine's arrest in 1873, Louis Riel having taken refuge in the United States. Lord Dufferin, taking a role in "this most thorny business," commuted Lépine's death sentence to two years with loss of civil rights. Lépine died in Saskatchewan in 1923 at the age of eighty-three.

basic lessons of staying alive. On this little patrol the old hand was Sam Steele who'd marched west with Wolseley's Expeditionary Force of 1870. Each afternoon the fourteen men stopped an hour before dark, tended their horses and sled dogs, cut piles of firewood, shovelled a clearing, spread buffalo robes, wolfed down buffalo steak, bread and tea, then stretched out around the fire, as Steele wrote later, "like herrings in a barrel, and slept well."

They reached Tail Creek after dark one night. It seemed deserted. They prowled through town, calling out, rapping on doors, peeking in. Where were all the people? Suddenly, over a chorus of howling dogs, they heard a screech of fiddles and a whoop of voices. They traced it to a large cabin and a rollicking wedding dance the like of which polite society in Montreal, Toronto or even Brockville had never seen.

a flash of scarlet

When Steele and Jarvis strode in that night the crowd was stomping through "Lord Macdonald's Reel." The room hushed and, while the dust settled, the Métis coolly sized up these tall, moustached, official-looking white men. Then the police loosened their outer coats and showed a flash of scarlet. "Bienvenu! Welcome!" Already Tail Creek knew and respected what the redcoats stood for; the Métis liked a drink but not the poisonous soul-destroying stuff of the whisky traders. That night the Mounties dined sumptuously on bannock, buffalo tongue, tinned fruit and the favourite non-alcoholic beverage of the West — strong tea.

They stayed four days, making friends and gathering gossip. The whisky traders never showed up but the Police later established a Tail Creek detachment: three log buildings and a stockade with a handful of men to keep the peace. Like most Eastern Canadians, the Mounties had scarcely heard of the Métis before Riel. To them the West had been as far-off and forbidding as the moon.

thousands of carcasses

The West was ten days or a fortnight away from Ontario by horse, steamer and railway through the United States. Dispatches by telegraph were few and often garbled. Only the priests, traders and Mounties, at first hand, developed sympathy for these displaced people. They found the Métis law-abiding, give or take a few fist fights, a people who only wanted a bit of country for themselves.

By 1876 the slaughter of the buffalo was completely out of hand. In the United States, settlers, surveyors, ranchers, hired hunters like Bill Cody and thrill-seekers popping away from trains left thousands of rotting carcasses. Most took only the tongues and hides or no meat at all. The Union Pacific Railway now ran through the American West and, because buffalo rarely would cross the rails, prevented some herds from moving north to the relative safety of Canada. The United States Army joined in the hunt deciding that, if it couldn't defeat the war-like Sioux, it would starve them into submission.

Canadian officialdom in 1877 belatedly outlawed the practice of driving buffalo over cliffs or into ambush, but even that law was repealed the next year. Then the Army, aided by "mysterious" grass fires all along the boundary, trapped the last herds during a migration south. The buffalo stopped at the burned earth, pathetic, puzzled, harmless creatures, and turned back to the final massacre.

Fire wiped out Tail Creek Town, too. One of the galloping prairie fires that seared the West, year after year, raced through Tail Creek in 1878, driving hordes of terrified wild animals ahead of it, leaving only one blackened cabin and a few stone chimneys on the site. But the Métis had already left and there was no point in rebuilding. The buffalo were almost gone, and so was the wild free West. In a little while the prairie silently erased all signs of Tail Creek Town from the face of the earth.

* * *

Hand-in-hand with settlement and the slaughter of the buffalo came the penning-up of the Indians. Seven successive treaty settlements in the seventies consigned all the Prairie Indians to reservations. One of the most significant was Treaty Six, embracing the Plains Cree nation and 120,000 square miles of fertile land. From verbatim accounts we know that this is how it was at Fort Carlton, north of what is now Saskatoon, on the days of August 18 – 26, 1876.

* * *

When the first light filtered through his tipi smokehole, the lesser chief Nah-wee-kah-nick-kah-oo-tah-mah-hote (Strike Him on the Back, in white man's language), crawled outdoors, yawned and studied this first day of the treaty talks. Sun, warmly rising. Sky, deep-water blue. Smoke from 250 Cree tipis rising straight up. His three wives were already kindling fire, heating tea and cooking bacon in battered copper pots. He stretched and yawned again, an aging man but the dark eyes still keen, the hair still black, the brown body, clad only in breechcloth and moccasins, still hard.

He sniffed, listened, looked. Smoke, rawhide, unwashed flesh, horse manure, dogs, the soft perfume of ripening grass. Barking, stamping hooves, a child's cry, a growing rumble of male voices. Buffalo-hide tipis in little clusters, their crossed-stick peaks mingling with thickets of willow and poplar on the meadow. Red River carts or travois hauled up beside each tipi. And beyond,

While Canada was still buying the West from the Indians, the North American Boundary Commission was at work from 1872 to 1875 staking out the limits of the 49th parallel. These official photographers of the Royal Engineers are preparing their wet-plate equipment.

Blackfoot Indians encircle lodges erected for the Sun Dance, a religious ceremony of initiation into manhood. In 1877 the Blackfoot tribes ceded title to their lands by formal treaty.

a troubling sight—the daytime tent of the Queen's Chief, the man called Governor Morris.

Strike Him on the Back squatted by the fire, taking food before the women and four children. This much was good: white men's rations were free during the treaty talks. There was not much fresh meat now. Life had been so good and simple, a little while ago. Eat, sleep, take a woman, fight the Blackfoot, hunt the buffalo that were thick as the grass itself. Then the whites came, killing, killing, killing, leaving the meat, taking only the hides and tongues. What could a Cree do against them? A few days before, some Saulteaux had come to the Cree at the North Saskatchewan River saying, "Help us stop the Queen's Chief at the crossing." The Cree replied, "Can you stop the flow of that river?" "No." "Then no more can you stop the coming of the white man." It was true. They could only bargain now, his own small band of seventy-eight; the bigger bands of leading chiefs Mist-ow-asis (Big Child) and Ah-tuck-uk-koop (Star Blanket); other bands, nearly two thousand Cree in all, come to negotiate a new way of life.

the pipe of peace

Strike Him on the Back pulled on leggings of soft cow-buffalo, fringed and trimmed with beads, and laced them to his belt thongs. Next, a white man's striped shirt, from the Bay post. Then a blue blanket, necklace of teeth and claws, heavily beaded pouch. He must look like a chief, for he had important duties to perform.

The camp was full of noise now. Shouting, haggling traders come from Fort Carlton two miles away. Crackling Winchesters and flint-locks. Thump-thump-thump of the little flat rawhide-covered drums. Blood-curdling cries of twenty young braves, feathered and painted, making wild practice runs on ponies for the show they would give the Governor.

Then all eight chiefs, the councillors and medicine men moved solemnly to sit in a semicircle on buffalo robes, facing that great white tent. Now! Strike Him on the Back stood with the pipe – long, painted, tasselled, bowl of soft stone – and slowly carried it before the others. South, west, north, east, he raised it high. He passed it to a young warrior who, with a shrill cry, began the Pipe Stem Dance. The chiefs joined in, then the councillors: a slow shuffling step, the whole camp chanting, the drums thumping, thumping.

the Queen's flag

Governor Morris came out: a man with wise eyes, dazzling blue tunic with gold trim, and a cocked hat. He sat on a chair before a table placed on a red carpet. On either side, his fellow commissioners: a Hudson's Bay factor named Christie and a huge Métis from Manitoba, McKay. Flanking them, two mounted ranks of Police, helmets like snow, their scarlet tunics a joy to a Cree's eye. Up the flagpole went the Queen's flag – red, white, blue. The white men were making a good show. Now it was the Cree's turn.

The young men broke into their gallop, wild, reckless, shooting, whooping. *See, white men? None can ride like the Cree!* Now Strike Him on the Back approached with the pipe. The commissioners stroked it. Good! They had accepted the friendship of the Cree nation. Up stepped Peter Erasmus, of Danish father and Cree mother, long acquainted with white men and their words. He introduced the chiefs. The Governor clasped each hand, white man's fashion.

There was a hush. The Governor spoke, pausing often for the little bursts of Cree translation. "My Indian brothers," he said, "I have shaken hands with a few of you. I shake hands with all of you in my heart. God has given us a good day. I trust his eye is upon us and that what we do is for the benefit of his children. You are like me and my friends – children of the Queen. We are of the same blood. The same God made us and the same Queen rules over us."

not one but many Spirits

Strike Him on the Back wrestled with these thoughts. If the whites were of the same blood, why were they white, and why did they so often cheat their dark brothers? And this God, so often praised by the mission men, was impossible to understand. It was well known there were not one but many Spirits: Sun, Sky, Earth, Rock, Moon, Wind, in that order.

As for this Queen, what was she? A woman's place was fetching water, tending children, cooking meat, scraping hides, making herself available to her man at night, always taking orders. Yet this Queen ruled armies, Police, even the Governor. Was she a Spirit? Perhaps a relative of the God? Evidently she was kind. Not long ago, the Governor was saying, some Indians from the East were taken across the great water and "the Queen said, 'I want to see my red children' and took their hands and gave them her picture and sent them away happy with her goodness."

Now the Governor spoke of other treaties already signed and how happy other Indians were. The Cree exchanged glances. This was known to be untrue. Two summers before in the treaty at Fort Qu'Appelle, a Cree chief called The Gambler had quarrelled with this same Governor. The Bay Company had stolen from the Indians "the earth, trees, grass, stones, all that which I see with my eyes," The Gambler cried. Not so, the Governor had argued; the Great Spirit intended those things for all men.

But it was so. The Indian had been here first – did that not mean that all this land belonged to the Indian? Today the Governor was

James McKay
Métis Commissioner

"The Hon. James McKay, M.P., has been a mighty hunter in his day, but as he now weighs 320 lbs., he leads a quieter though still a very active life. He is a half-breed . . . and he speaks the three languages." Thus Lady Dufferin described the 'boss' of their entourage on a Manitoba tour in 1877. The former H.B.C. guide was interpreter and go-between during the Indian treaty talks. From 1874 to 1878, he was provincial minister of agriculture for Manitoba.

**Alexander Morris
The Man Who Made the Treaties**

The first arts graduate of McGill University, Alexander Morris entered politics becoming minister of inland revenue for John A. Macdonald in 1869. Three years later he was appointed Manitoba's first chief justice, a post he gave up to become lieutenant-governor of Manitoba and the North-West Territories from 1872 to 1877. His book, *The Treaties of Canada with the Indians of the North-West*, published in 1880, offers a remarkable word-by-word account of the procedures leading up to the Indian treaties.

hurrying past such arguments: "The day is passing, I want you to think of my words. What we will do is not for today or tomorrow only. It is to last as long as that sun shines and yonder river flows. I thank you for the respectful attention you have given me."

Good! One did not rush everything into a day. The chiefs retired to smoke and plan. Tomorrow, surely, there would be offers of gifts, in exchange for land. "A summer ago the white men spoke of gifts to Big Bear," a councillor reminded them. "To them Big Bear said, 'We want none of the Queen's presents. We set a fox trap, we scatter pieces of meat all around, but when the fox gets into the trap we knock him on the head. We want no bait.'" The chiefs grunted. They knew Big Bear, a Saulteaux in their territory, a trouble-maker but a feared and powerful medicine man. Still, Big Bear was wrong. The Cree had to sign and should receive presents. There should be help in times of sickness like the one that, six summers ago, left pocked faces and heaps of rotting Cree bodies. Protection from men who sold the fiery water that turned some of their sons crazy. Protection from others who spread wolf poison that also killed dogs, deer, horses, buffalo. All these things and more must be asked for.

"Think of these words"

Three days slipped by. A Police band played: neat shiny music that marched in straight orderly lines like white soldiers. The Governor spoke more fine words: how a new bright sky stretched before the Indians; how each band would have its "reserve" of land with tools, seeds, oxen. Big Child clasped the Governor's hand, replying, "I ask this much, that we go and think of these words." The Governor, swallowing his disappointment, remembered to think like a Cree: "Try to understand what is in my heart toward you."

On the white man's Sunday, Strike Him on the Back listened to a reverend from the thing called Church of England tell in Cree how his god punished evil-doers. That night the drums thumped and the people danced at a happy little feast. In the morning everyone was tired so Big Child sent word that the Cree, having not yet held council out of respect for the Governor's Sunday, needed another day.

a new way of life

On the white man's Tuesday, the Governor said, "Indian children of the Queen, I have not hurried you. You have had two days to think. Now I wish to hear you. My ears are open." Up stepped Poundmaker, tall and handsome, not yet a chief but much admired and famed as a maker of traps for catching buffalo. His deep expressive voice circled around his subject, in Indian fashion: the people were glad to be told how to live by their own work but they would need much help in every way. "We do not want to be too greedy," chimed in the Badger. "When we settle on the reserves, it is there we want your aid in case of troubles seen and not seen in the future."

Trust the Queen, replied the Governor. Last winter when Indians were starving because the grasshoppers ate their crops, the good Queen sent money even though it had not been promised. "We have not come to deceive you, we have not come here to rob you," the Métis Commissioner McKay added. "We have not come here to take away anything that belongs to you." *But you have come to take our land!*

The Badger tried again: "I do not want you to feed me every day, you must not understand that from what I have said. When we commence to settle down on the ground, it is then we want your help." But there would be seed for the Cree to plant, the Governor repeated stubbornly.

This strange matter of farming still troubled the Cree, added Star Blanket. They must have another afternoon for more discussion. Angry now, the Governor granted one last day. Now the Cree returned to their tipis. No point in more delay. That night they drew the list of requests. An ox, a cow, four hoes, two spades, two scythes, a whetstone for each family. Two axes, two hay forks, two reaping hooks, one plough, one harrow for every three families. A chest of tools for each chief. Seed. Help for the poor, blind and lame. A minister and a school teacher. No firewater to be sold to the Indians. Freedom to hunt as they pleased. A bear, two sows, one horse, harness and a wagon for each chief. Medicine. And a pledge that the Indians would not be forced to fight in the Queen's wars.

the land is wide

In the morning, after Peter Erasmus had read the requests, Strike Him on the Back rose to speak, his only long speech of the treaty days, a speech bursting from the heart.

"Pity the voice of the Indian!" he cried. "If you grant what we request, the sound will echo through the land. Open the way. I speak for the children, that they may be glad. The land is wide, there is plenty of room." Peter Erasmus hurried to keep up with the translation. "My mouth is full of milk, I am only as a suckling child. I am glad on the manner in which I was brought up but let us now stand in the light of day to see our way on this earth. Long ago it was good. I wish the same were back again. But now the law has come. What the God has said, and our mother here . . ." he stamped on the earth, ". . . and these our brethren, let it be so." A chorus of approval welled up from the camp. A good speech. *We are sad and confused*, it tried to say. *But we will try your way if you will help us.*

The Governor waited for silence. "You are like other Indians I have met, you can ask very well," he said wearily. "You are right in asking, though, because you are saying what is in your minds." He spoke to the other commissioners. Then he turned back, friendly but stern, no longer their brother but a white man speaking to children. "I am ready now to answer you, but understand well, it is not to be talked backwards and forwards. I am not going to act like a man bargaining for a horse. My answer will be a final one."

The tribe would get $1,000 a year for three years to help them start farming; no other treaty Indians had received so much. All tools and implements were granted. There would be teachers. The churches would send missionaries. The Queen could not care for the poor, but if they worked hard the Indians would be able to care for their own. The Police would prevent the selling of firewater; already they had nearly stopped it. The Cree would be free to hunt, if they did not destroy the farmers' crops. Free medicine, yes. No, the Queen would not make them fight, if they did not want to fight. And for each band: four oxen, six cows, a boar, a bull, two pigs. Now! Would they take the Queen's gifts?

"Now I ask my people," cried Star Blanket, "those that are in favour of the offer, say so!" A roar of approval. But Poundmaker held back; he wanted more explanation; he was confused; he did not know how to build a house. One councillor, Joseph Thoma, was even more outspoken: each headman should have a horse too; the whites should build the Indian houses; each chief and headman should have a gun. The Governor was showing anger again, and quickly the other Cree shouted Thoma down. One by one, they put an *X* beside each name on the roll of white man's paper. The last to sign was Strike Him on the Back.

In the morning the Governor gave each chief a scarlet tunic, a black top hat with gold band, a flag

Reading the first of the Western Indian Treaties in Manitoba in 1871.

and a silver medal bearing a picture of the great Queen. Then he spoke sharply to a little group of Saulteaux who stubbornly stood aloof from the proceedings. Were they the ones who had wanted to stop him from crossing the river? And had they urged the Cree not to accept the treaty?

It was true, admitted their spokesman, Nus-was-oo-wah-tum, and added things no Cree had dared say: "He that made us provided everything for our way of living. I am not tired of it. And now that you come and stand on this our earth, I do not understand. I see dimly what you are doing and I find fault with some of it. That is why I stand back. Through what you have done you have cheated my kinsmen."

The Governor's temper flared. "I will not sit and hear such words! Who are you? You tell me the Queen has cheated you. It is not so! You say we have the best of the bargains; you know it is not so! If you have any requests to make in respectful manner, I am ready to hear!" But the Saulteaux turned away. "The white man is not my master."

Strike Him on the Back pondered those words all that day and the next, as the Cree lined up for treaty money (for himself and family of seven: $109). It troubled him still, on the farewell morning, August 26, when all the Cree, headed by chiefs in new hats, coats and medals, went to Fort Carlton to hear the Governor's last speech and obediently give three white man's cheers for him, for the Queen, for the Police – all the new masters.

Accepting the treaty was right, surely? No use fighting the white man; no use letting the children starve. But Strike Him on the Back may have dimly sensed that a single leap from spear to plough was impossible; that he and his family were now neither free Indian nor full Canadian; that wise Poundmaker, angry Big Bear, yes even reluctant Strike Him on the Back, would rise eight years hence for one more futile fight against the whites. And Treaty Number Six, like all the treaties, would leave a bitter taste for generations.

This quiet scene of a lone Sarcee encamped with his wife would be interrupted a few years hence by prairie unrest in the eighties.

CHAPTER FIVE

The Man in the Corner Store

Barter was the normal, everyday method of doing business. Farmers had little or no cash.

C.L. Burton, *A Sense of Urgency*

For the overworked, underpaid, long-suffering male there was always *one* refuge, one home away from home, one haven of warmth, companionship and gossip that didn't cost a cent or send him home blind drunk. When nagging wife, whining children, tyrannical boss, the whole intolerable world closed in on him, he could always flee to the general store.

Every Canadian hamlet had one; every town had several; every city had dozens and, with one notable exception, they were the same. The general store was a cluttered, intricate, interesting place, redolent with cheese, leather, ham, coffee, molasses, coal-oil, dried fish, vinegar and a thousand other scents, all blended by an alchemy no scientist will ever match, a glorious tantalizing assault on the nostrils.

Typically, it was about twenty by thirty feet with a couple of windows facing the street and two doors at the back. One led to the storeroom where barrels of flour, butter and pork, kegs of nails and maybe a coffin or two were kept. The other opened on the office where friends of the storekeeper might find a hand of euchre or a nip of cider. It was not just a grocery store, but a drapery, ironmongery, confectionery, hardware and dry-goods store. It sold dishes, rope, petroleum, lollipops, ribbons, patent medicine, horehound drops, dresses, pickled herring, jawbreakers, copper foot-warmers, corset stays, boots, nails, crocks, churns, curry combs, buggy whips, lanterns and cowbells.

Packaged goods were unknown, so sugar came in twenty-pound cones with cutters to snip off your order. Cheese was in enormous golden cartwheels. Coffee beans were ground on the spot. Molasses came by the puncheon. Bulk items such as beans were ladled from bins and weighed on the balance scale. "Strictly fresh" eggs came in baskets lined with buckwheat hulls. A really up-to-date store had some of the new-fangled canned goods: rabbit, clams, scallops or blueberries.

But this was only the mercantile side of the business. In its role as community centre, the store had a squat black iron stove, a half-dozen chairs, two counters running along each side of the building and an open cracker barrel. The choice chairs by the stove were, by common assent, yielded to the leading men of the community. Here they, and the other ranks perched on the counter, smoked, whittled, munched crackers, played checkers, gossiped, argued, chewed tobacco or spruce gum and spat with sizzling accuracy against the glowing red belly of the stove.

The best times were when a travelling salesman or drummer came in by train, stage or buggy with

THE WORLD'S GREATEST SEWING MACHINE NEW HOME

Spencer Matheson,
Waterloo, P. Q.

The lock-stitch sewing machine was just one of the popular items that the general store kept in stock.

**Timothy Eaton
Revolutionary Merchandiser**

The level gaze of Irish-born Timothy Eaton, does not bespeak an innovative genius. But his concept of "goods for cash only" struck a fatal blow at the common practice of credit and barter. Within a few decades, Eaton had expanded from a struggling drygoods store to a major department store shipping goods across Canada. By 1887 he had instituted that national consumers' bible, Eaton's Catalogue, used from coast to coast as almanac, buyers' guide, fashion arbiter, or model for eager do-it-yourselfers.

news of the outside world. A business newspaper defined the commercial traveller of the 1870s as:

A man of good morals, good habits and good manners. He should have a good business training, a technical knowledge of the particular branch which he is employed in. He needs to be a judge of character, of sufficient shrewdness not to be outwitted by the keen close buyers and cunning deadbeats he is sure to encounter. He ought to possess a knowledge of the country through which he travels, its products and its capacities.

A good ear for gossip helped, too. The gang around the store expected it. None of the hangers-on was under obligation to purchase. Nobody told them to buy or get out. The storekeeper enjoyed their company and, as a local entrepreneur (maybe doubling as banker or dealer in mortgages), he appreciated the value of public relations.

Anyway, "buying" was a misnomer. Those were the days of credit and barter, especially in the country. Customers rarely parted with real money. When a farmer drove to town on market day, he might bring eggs, pork, butter or potatoes to swap for axes, pots, saws or rope. More often he bought on credit. In either case, like Canadian shoppers everywhere, he never dreamed of paying the asking price. He knew it was set unduly high and the storekeeper expected to be "dickered" down. It was a game everyone played and nearly everyone lost.

a quaint system

Starting a store was easy and looked like quick money. Many men left their farms to try it, opened with loss-leader prices and went broke immediately. Others survived the initial period but eventually ruined themselves by extending credit for from three months to two years. The customers lived in alternate states of euphoria and sheer panic, when

as much as two years' reckoning of their extravagance finally arrived.

Into this quaint but chaotic system came Timothy Eaton, a balding square-bearded Irishman of thirty-five with stern habits and a level gaze that made junior clerks shuffle nervously. He neither smoked, drank, danced nor played cards. He was scrupulously honest and he'd learned storekeeping the hard way: first as an apprentice in Ireland, where he slept under the counter and rose at five every morning; then as a clerk and later as a store-owner in small Ontario towns where he discovered the pitfalls of barter. Eaton came out of all this with a revolutionary idea: he intended to run a store with no credit and fixed prices.

the glittering thoroughfare

He chose to try it in Toronto, a fast-growing place full of Tories, churches, bars, Orangemen, Methodists and other merchants. Its population of 56,000 sprawled from the Ontario Lunatic Asylum on the west to east of the Don river and north as far as the village of Yorkville. Its wholesale district ran along Front Street, close to railways and the waterfront. Its fashionable homes were on Jarvis Street. But for a merchant there was only one *good* place to be – King Street.

King was the glittering thoroughfare of commerce and fashion. Its buildings were grander than those on nearby Yonge, its shops were larger and swankier. "King Street is honoured by the daily presence of the aristocracy while Yonge is given over to the business of the middle class and the beggar," reported an 1870 writer for the *Canadian Illustrated News*. "Amid the upper classes there is a performance that goes on daily, known as 'doing King.' It consists principally of marching up and down a certain part of that street at a certain hour, performing as it were 'kowtow' to the goddess of fashion."

DICKERING DOWN AT THE STORE

Frank Laumeister's Victoria customers shop here mainly because of the meat.

Goods of every description line all available shelves of the general store.

Victoria's Victoria House recognizes that window dressing will increase sales.

Chairs, tables, desks and dressers ready for markets in Southwestern Ontario.

A team of oxen strain past St. Crispins' shoe mart on house-moving day in Yarmouth, N.S.

Timothy Eaton couldn't afford to buy or even rent on King Street, but he shrewdly leased the ground floor of a building on the fringe of the favoured district at the corner of Yonge and Queen Streets. Most of residential Toronto lay immediately north. A horse-drawn streetcar (fare: five cents) passed his door every half-hour. People bound for the King Street stores had to go by Eaton's, and Timothy vowed he'd pull them in.

for cash only

First he made Toronto take notice with his opening advertisement in the *Globe* in the final days of 1869. It read in part:

> *NEW DRY GOODS BUSINESS!*
> *T. Eaton & Co.*
> *Have purchased from Mr. James Jennings,*
> *his ENTIRE STOCK OF DRY GOODS*
> *At a very considerable reduction from the cost price which amounts to several thousand dollars, every dollar of which they propose to give to those customers who may favour them with their patronage.*

It went on to list the bargains – four thousand yards of wincey (light-weight cotton cloth) at five cents per yard, fancy dress goods at ten cents per yard, mourning goods and flannels at the same rates, all millinery goods at half the market price. Then Eaton tossed in his bombshell:

> *We propose to sell our goods for CASH ONLY. In selling goods to have only one price. We invite an examination of our stock and to all we offer our best services.*

One price! His rivals scoffed and spread rumours that Eaton would go broke. But he didn't. His twenty-four-by-sixty-foot store had two multi-pane show-windows and he filled those windows with tempting bargains: baskets heaped with

The Golden Griffin, one of Eaton's dry goods competitors on King Street, Toronto.

thread at one cent a spool and neckties at five cents each; folds of merino and cashmere suspended from nails; parasols arranged in jaunty poses; and always the price tag prominently shown.

He introduced another startling idea: "Goods satisfactory or your money refunded." To that point in Canadian mercantile history, a merchant's responsibility ended when he sold an article. In some shops, customers could get an exchange but never a refund. Yet this man Eaton, if you weren't satisfied, actually gave your money back! At first the customers were flabbergasted and sometimes critical. "I have accounts at every *other* store," they'd complain when asked for cash. But Eaton's merchandise, prices and service were irresistible. Where else could you get women's genuine linen handkerchiefs at ten cents each? Or waterproof tweeds for $1.20 a yard, regular $1.75? If a customer was dissatisfied, the staff (two men, a woman and a boy) were under strict instructions to report it immediately to Mr. Eaton, who personally tried to remedy the problem before the shopper got away.

a Scot named Simpson

He trained his staff to be painfully honest, even if it meant losing a sale. Once he overheard a clerk describe a certain material as all wool. "No, madam," Eaton interrupted. "It is half cotton." Torontonians began to believe Eaton's claim that a child could safely shop in his store. In 1872 the *Ontario Workman*, a labour newspaper, supported their advertiser with the compliment:

When Mr. Eaton placards the city that he has goods and cheap dresses, shawls, blankets or anything else in his line of business you will invariably, on visiting his store, find him ready and prepared to sell just as he has advertised to do. Mechanics and their families in want of drygoods are recommended to make Mr. Eaton an

early call and we can assure them that they will be well repaid for so doing.

The man in the corner store was surrounded by competition. A dozen drygoods stores operated within a block or two, including a new one run by a Scot named Robert Simpson. Often they waged fierce battles of the show-windows: if Eaton showed a certain print at three and a half cents a yard, a competitor would display it at three cents. Times were becoming hard, too – during the depression years of the seventies, many Canadian businesses failed. And there were all the usual hazards of storekeeping anywhere, anytime; as Eaton disconsolately wrote his brother one day, "My sales not so good. . . . Our ladies won't come out while it rains."

the hour-glass shape

But Eaton survived, partly because he applied his own distinctive touch to everything. Through the decade, for example, he did his overseas buying personally and from the best European manufacturers. His clothes were not necessarily high fashion but a lady outfitted at Eaton's was thoroughly up to date. In other words, her silhouette looked like the town firebell.

In all but the warmest weather she wore flannel underwear with high neckline and long sleeves. Her stockings were balbriggan or cashmere. She wore a corset whether she needed it or not, and its iron grip moulded her into the approved hour-glass shape. Corsets were fortified with whalebone until, at the end of the seventies, one Dr. Warner introduced Coraline stays made from plant fibre. As Dr. Warner pointed out,

It CANNOT be broken. A REWARD OF $10 will be paid for every strip of Coraline which breaks with four months' ordinary wear in a corset. It is more pliable than whalebone and so adapts itself more readily to the movements of the body.

**Robert Simpson
A Friendly Rival**

Young Robert Simpson emigrated from Scotland to Canada in 1855 to work in and operate a Newmarket drygoods store. His 1872 move to Toronto brought him into competition with Eaton. Their enterprises developed a friendly but lasting rivalry as they jockied for the best store frontage in the Yonge-Queen Streets vicinity. In 1883 when Eaton moved north of Queen, Simpson took over the south-west corner location, and the two stores grew in tandem through the next two decades, becoming inter-twined in common parlance.

63

A bold copy-writer himself, Robert Simpson early incorporated the Canadian ensign, slashed with his name, as his advertising logo.

SOUTH-WEST CORNER

YONGE AND QUEEN.

R. SIMPSON

TREMENDOUS
—:SUMMER:—
GLOSING-OUT SALE

Nearly Half a Million Dollars Worth ($500,-
000) of Staple and Fancy Dry Goods to be
cleared before the 1st of October.

R. SIMPSON

South-West Corner Yonge and Queen,
TORONTO. - - ONTARIO.

The corset was topped with as many as four petticoats. Then came a gown of cashmere, gauze, tarlatan, muslin, wincey, *barège* or poplin, with assorted frills, lace or trim depending on season or fashion. It had a long close-fitting bodice and a blossoming floor-length skirt puffed out by sheer force of petticoat. Over the shoulders went a paletot, sacque or mantelet – small coats of various kinds. Then a little pancake of a bonnet or a hat (hats with feathers were in fashion by 1875) and, finally, gloves. No lady worthy of the name would appear on the street or at a dance without gloves.

An Eaton's-equipped man, if he were a bit of a swell, stepped out in frock-coat, double-breasted waistcoat, striped trousers, wing collar, floppy cravat and silk hat. There was even a modest demand for men's corsets, mostly from army officers who sought to move their sagging chests back up under their medals.

bargains in bold type

Buying merchandise was just one of a multitude of chores Eaton assigned to himself. He kept a sharp eye on wholesalers who were not above trying to con the local merchants. In those days ship compartments were not thoroughly watertight, and wet goods were sold off at "wet sales." Some ingenious wholesalers were always producing water-damaged stock – actually old merchandise they'd carefully soaked in barrels of salt water. Eaton also supervised the distribution of forty thousand handbills a month. These, his chief advertising medium, shouted the bargains in bold type. They were to be folded in a prescribed manner and tucked firmly under householders' doors, and the small delivery boy knew Eaton was liable to run a spot-check anytime.

Eaton also expected his employees to be absolutely punctual, a personal habit dating from his own apprenticeship when once he was left to walk

nine miles home because, although in sight, he was not actually *at* an appointed meeting-place when his boss drove by. Yet Eaton was in the forefront of employers by his treatment of his staff. In the beginning they, like all store employees, worked from eight in the morning to ten at night, five days a week and to midnight on Saturdays, but they received top wages for the times. The small boy who took down the shutters in the morning, put them up at night and did errands in between earned $1.50 a week. The two male clerks earned $8 each a week; the woman, $4.

Unlike other shopkeepers, Eaton gave them time off during the day to keep them fresh for evening work, paid bonuses for the most sales and treated everyone to pork pies and coffee on Saturday night. When an employee was ill, Eaton's wife, Margaret, generally took flowers or home-made goodies to their house. When a junior employee said he was going to rent a boat to watch the mighty sculler, Ned Hanlan, row a race in the bay, Eaton pressed $10, a princely sum, into his hand to help him *buy* his own boat. Late in the seventies, Eaton introduced the 6:00 P.M. closing time, five days a week.

the Yonge-Queen stop

By then Toronto was a city of 86,000 and Eaton had a staff of twenty. His little store had stretched back another forty feet to accommodate carpets, oilcloth, blankets and quilts. One of the new coal furnaces replaced the original box stove. He took over the building's second floor for a millinery showroom where, after his wife talked him into it, he provided two hand mirrors so women customers could examine the backs of their heads as well as the fronts. A man in a pony cart whisked around town on twice-a-day deliveries. By the end of the decade Eaton was selling $12,000 worth of goods a month – and the streetcar men automatically called out "Eaton's" at the Yonge-Queen stop.

So eminently successful was the Eaton cash-and-fair-play method that others began to adopt it. The *Monetary Times,* reporting on several stores that had tried it successfully, added, "This system of wholesale country credit is rotten to the core and we must get rid of it if we are to abandon hard times and chronic failures."

In rural areas the old ways lingered on; stores were still occasional social centres and still offered modified credit. But the man at the corner of Yonge and Queen had established an irrevocable trend. The old general store, so dear to the heart and so disastrous to the pocketbook, would soon be eclipsed by the new store that provided *everything* a family needed – from patent medicines to farm machinery – neatly organized in departments.

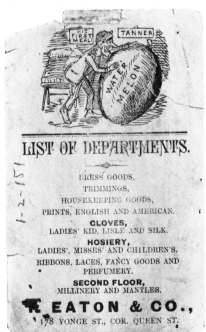

It was Mrs. Eaton who suggested the millinery showroom be added to the growing "list of departments" (above). The charming trade card (right) announced Eaton's move to larger quarters north of Queen Street in August 1883.

Innocent Soft Sell

Trade cards had been common advertising items since the early 1800s. Mid-century developments in colour lithography sparked an avalanche of these gay and glorious cards in the 1870s and 1880s. Avid collectors filled albums, swapped duplicates and framed their favourites to hang in parlour or kitchen. A company often reserved only a small corner to print its name.

Guelph's Bell Organ Company used a patriotic sales pitch.

A & P "eggspatiated" a curious conundrum for its customers.

Toronto's fashionable Victoria Tea House used a sweet lass for its advertising.

McMurray & Co. of Halifax took to barn-yard comedy to sell goods.

No Canadian home was complete without a Domestic sewing machine.

Wheeler & Wilson's latest time-saving invention delighted these ladies.

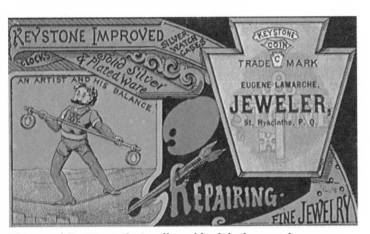

This proud St.-Hyacinthe jeweller sold solid silver watch cases.

John Russell & Co. shaped its advertising to drum-up more business.

CHAPTER SIX

How We Wooed an Island Paradise

We have sold our noble little ship, and she now stands stripped of all [her] glory. . . .

A.E.C. Holland, opponent of Confederation, P.E.I., 1873

Snug, fertile little Prince Edward Island. Red clay cliffs, winding roads, hazy green hills, tidy farmhouses, all as purely perfect as the prize-winning sampler at the Charlottetown Wesleyan Church bazaar. What an asset this island would be to the new nation! Except that Islanders don't want any part of Canada. They have no inkling, here in 1870, that within three years they will be hauled into Confederation aboard that most marvellous plaything of their time – the railway train. Right now they see no point in becoming just another province, dependent, heavily taxed and the smallest at that. Who needs Canada? Why spoil Paradise?

They have a weathered outdoor look, most of these ninety-four thousand Islanders. Nine-tenths of them live on farms or in backcountry villages. They hew and hammer trees into sailing ships, haul in bulging nets of cod, herring, mackerel, halibut and lobster. They parlay that red earth into wheat, barley, potatoes and oats. Many of them are Scots. Here in Paradise, dealing with a Scot, you must *really* offer bargains. Elsewhere you advertise a farm in barest terms. Here you must add that it is "within one mile of a good

shooting place; plenty of seaweed within a mile; two hundred loads of manure on the farm." Or you must explain that your eighty-seven acres include good well, five-bedroom house, forty-foot barn and all necessary outbuildings for £450 (about $2,200; Prince Edward Island is still on pound sterling), *and* all furniture, guns, books, china and custom-made piano at cost.

There is, unfortunately, a tendency for Islanders to be bamboozled by city men with "bargains" in goods or health. It seems that numerous country folk have recently been conned into buying clocks at eight pounds sterling apiece, about five times their value. Patent-medicine vendors, knowing the Islanders' suspicion of professional men, are helpfully urging them to avoid "the hieroglyphics of a doctor's prescription" and buy Morse's Indian Root Pills ("Nine times out of ten a better remedy than most doctors give"). And naturally, considering the price, any right-thinking Islander is going to save his wife from "insanity, fits, heart disease, rush of blood to the head, vomiting of blood, weakness, lowness of spirits, languor, loss of appetite, consumption and rapid decline" by daily plying her with two to six of Radway's Pills and immersing her feet in Radway's Renovating Solvent.

All right, maybe Islanders do get hooked on mainlanders' bargains. But nobody will ever catch them off-base on any aspect of farming. The

Sydney P. Hall, an artist for the London *Graphic, sketched a typical Islander in 1878. He must have been Scottish, a farmer and God-fearing.*

Opposite page: Loading Bricks, *an oil sketch by Robert Harris, the Island's own native artist.*

THE SPLENDID HORSE.

YOUNG NETHERBY !

WILL STAND FOR MARES THIS SEASON AS FOLLOWS.

Monday, May 4th, he wil leave his own stable, 3rd line, Esquesing, and proceed to G. Gibbs' Ballinafad, for noon ; thence to W. Neirs, 9th line Erin for night.

Tuesday, he will proceed to W. Chisholm's hotel Erin Village tor noon ; thence to Redrick's hotel Bellefountain, for night.

Wednesday, he will proceed to J. Silks' hotel, Cataract, for noon ; thence to the Dixie House, Alton for night

Thursday, he will proceed to G. Hurd's 10th line Erin for noon ; thence to G. Dent's hotel, Hillsburgh for night.

Friday he will proceed to John Burt's for noon ; thence to J. Fielding's Ospring for night.

Saturday, he will proceed to Acton, for noon ; thence to his own stable where he will remain till the following Monday.

PEDIGREE.---"Young Netherby" is a beautiful dark bay, 16 hands high 6 years old past. He was sired by Mr. Joseph Thompson's imported Netherby, dam by the imported Merry Farmer. Young Netherby took several First Prizes when a colt, at Whitby and other places, and took the second prize at the Rockwood and Milton shows. He has proved himself a sure foal getter, and has got more good stock than any horse travelling in the same section. One of his colts took the first prize at Guelph last year for a yearling colt, one took second prize at Milton and Rockwood, and first at Georgetown.

TERMS--Single Leap $4, to be paid at the time of servic · otherwise they will be charged as Season Mares. For the Season $6 to be paid on the last round. To insure a foal $8 to be paid on the 1st February 1875. Mares that are insured must be returned regularly to the horse, or they will be charged as season Mares· Persons disposing of their Mares before foaling time must pay for insurance whether in foal or not. Accidents at risk of owners. Groom's Fees 50 cts Cash down.

ROBERT GIBBONS, Proprietor & Groom.

Esquesing, May 1st, 1874.   Printed at the HERALD Office, Georgetown.

Netherby's owner arranged a hectic schedule of service for the young stud! Canadians of the 1870s lavished the same kind of adulation on horseflesh as their grandchildren do on horsepowe

newspapers are full of advice: how to breed pigs, protect cabbage, keep scythes sharp, care for suckling colts, destroy sow-thistle, raise carrots. If the Islander is Frederick Lepage, missing a long-horned brindle cow, he writes to the papers offering a "suitable" reward for her recovery. If the Islander is "Old Settler," *he* writes to remind everyone that Young Roland and Champion stand ready and willing at the government stud farm. Both will be "allowed to serve a limited number of good mares." Young Roland, a thoroughbred, is son and heir of Roland the celebrated racer, and Champion "bids fair to be the heaviest finest cart horse ever raised on the Island."

"Dexter's Wonderful Trot"

Islanders love horseflesh. Their favourite bit of newspaper science fiction is "Dexter's Wonderful Trot." Dexter, a horse, is hero of this long-running advertisement. The ad never changes yet never fails to thrill: how Dexter, fortified with Carlton's Condition Powders, trots the mile pulling a wagon in two minutes, twenty-one seconds; how Mr. Bonner, the only human in this little drama, cries "Up Dexter!" and the noble beast, despite a nasty headwind, finishes the last quarter in a "dart of electric speed."

There are about twenty-five thousand horses on the Island, causing some mainlanders to suggest that horses outnumber the people. This is not true, of course, but it is one of the typically snide remarks the Islanders have come to expect from Canadians.

Charlottetown is the most conservative spot on the American continent. Here may be heard the argument 'We have done without it hitherto, why should we want anything new?' Hence the traveller finds no coach or cab to meet him, no hotel worth the name to walk into, no pavement to walk on, no

accommodation of any sort. *The citizens are content to cart their water half a mile.*
Ottawa Citizen, *May 19, 1871*

It's a lie! Or, anyway, an exaggeration. Charlottetown has *some* hotels, for those not too fussy about where they sleep. And *some* boardwalks, even though an otherwise eulogistic local history reports that the sidewalks threaten to trip and throw the passerby. True, there isn't a single horse-cab in town. And yes, citizens' water is still hauled by cart from a spring to Charlottetown, but that's a temporary measure. Things will become much more up to date when the railroad arrives. (Did somebody mention a railroad?)

Meanwhile, Charlottetown isn't such an un-civilized place. There are regular lectures on topics like "The Causes of Earthquakes, Storms and Tidal Waves." There's regular ice delivery and mail delivery from the mainland three times a week. Moreover, it is a peaceful place, unruffled by violence at home or abroad. In early August, with Prussian cavalry five miles from Paris, the *Islander*'s front page ignores the war and reports on Cleaver's Carbolic Soap, a church bazaar, a new shipment of milk pans and butter crocks, and the feats of Fairlie's Little Wonder, a railway engine in Wales.

brass, bells and cow-catcher

Railway? There *is* a good deal of reference to trains now in the press. Articles explain the principle of horsepower. Advertisements shout "The Railway is coming!" It seems that, going into 1870, the government of Prince Edward Island was honour-bound not to enter Confederation without first seeking the voters' approval. But the government could and did go ahead and plan a railway all by itself. After all, every place should have a train, in the up-to-date seventies, and nearly every

Islanders welcomed a wide variety of touring entertainers at Charlottetown's Market Hall. The Sheppard Jubilee Singers from Virginia harmonized on its stage in July of 1875.

ALL ABOARD THE IRON HORSE

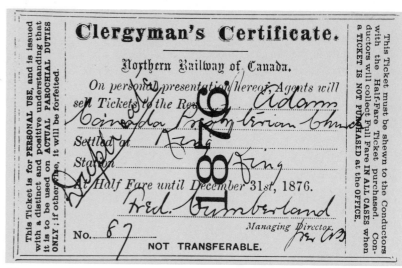

In an era when railways were big business, politicians received special treatment for patriotic service – or perhaps just for their patronage.

Clergymen also benefited from the charitable instincts of railway owners in a highly religious age. Note the warnings against abuse of privileges.

Rich panelling and drapery and comfortable armchairs provided the acme of elegance for the governor general.

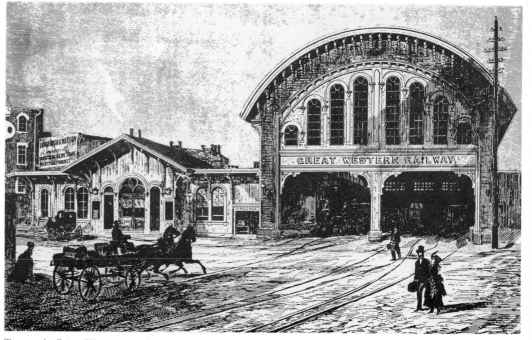

Toronto's Great Western Railway Station, at the foot of Yonge Street, was situated conveniently opposite the wharf where freight-laden steamers from Montreal docked.

While controversy raged over the routes and financing of the CPR, Central Canadians and Maritimers revelled in the dubious conveniences of established railways. The last stretches of the Intercolonial, completed in 1876, gave the nine-year-old nation a 700-mile rail link from her Atlantic ports to her agricultural heartland.

INTERCOLONIAL RAILWAY
⸎ CANADA ⸎
BETWEEN
Point Levi, Campbellton, Moncton,
SHEDIAC, PICTOU,
HALIFAX & ST. JOHN.

CLOSE CONNECTIONS MADE

At HALIFAX with First-Class Mail Steamers of the Montreal Ocean Steamship Company to and from LIVERPOOL, making the shortest ocean passage between the two Continents.

MAKING CONNECTIONS
During the Season of Navigation.

At CAMPBELLTON with Steamer "City of St. John," sailing Wednesday and Saturday Mornings for Paspebiac, Percé, Gaspé, &c., &c.

— AND AT —

POINTE DU CHÊNE with Steamers for Prince Edward Island,

Is supplied with First Class Equipments in every particular.

SMITH'S VACUUM BRAKES AND MILLER'S PLATFORMS
ON ALL PASSENGER CARS.

PULLMAN PALACE SLEEPING CARS RUN ON EXPRESS TRAINS BETWEEN

ST. JOHN, HALIFAX, QUEBEC AND MONTREAL.

Baggage checked through to all Principal Points in Canada and United States.

This Line offers superior facilities for SHIPMENTS OF FREIGHT to or from the Upper Provinces, the Gauge being the same as that of the Western Railways.

C. SCHREIBER,
Chief Engineer Govt. Railways in operation.

By 1879 the Intercolonial was advertising first class services – and Pullman Palace Sleeping Cars – but its trains seldom ran on time.

To complete the New Brunswick stretches of the Intercolonial in 1874, workers erected this bridge superstructure across the Miramichi.

Three railways – the Grand Trunk, the Great Western and the Northern – combined in 1873 for construction of a second Union Station in Toronto.

This 1874 handbill for Girard's magic show in Charlottetown's Market Hall also promised such "new and startling illusions" as Dancing Skeleton Twins.

place does. Canada has about five thousand miles of track and twenty or thirty different railway companies. There's talk of a line all the way to the Pacific. By 1876 the Intercolonial, will link the Maritimes to Quebec and Ontario. By 1878 even Winnipeg will have a rail hook-up with the United States. Prince Edward Island must not be left out.

Anyway, trains are an absolute delight with their brass, bells, cow-catcher and funnel-shaped smokestack billowing woodsmoke. They have crimson plush seats and oil-lamps in stained glass shades. The ride is rough, but not as bad as a stage coach, and you can actually sleep while travelling in the new Pullman cars, for only a dollar extra.

look out for the locomotive

Trains have a few faults. They're dirty: passengers are advised to carry flaxseeds to remove cinders from their eyes. They're chilly in winter, when they get stranded in snowbanks and the wood for the stoves in the coaches runs out. They're hot in summer because the windows are nailed shut to keep out sparks. They're scary when they clatter over frail bridges and crossings marked WHEN THE BELL RINGS LOOK OUT FOR THE LOCOMOTIVE Fighting for a place in the restaurant at station stops is as bruising as playing lacrosse against the Caughnawaga Indians. But it's rumoured that soon trains will have dining cars offering elegant meals at a mere seventy-five cents.

Most important, trains are fast, averaging twenty or thirty miles per hour, and can travel in most weather. This is what catches the Islanders' fancy. A railroad will be good for business. The autumn of 1870 points up the shortcomings of a non-railway economy. Heavy rains inundate the Island, turning clay roads to bogs. Ships wait empty at the wharves for their overseas cargoes.

The railroad would probably cost us some £30,000 a year. The savings to ordinary roads and

A Painter's Island

Tranquil Prince Edward Island was the inspiration for artist Robert Harris, its native son. Born in Wales in 1849, Harris grew up in P.E.I. and studied in London and Paris before settling in Montreal. But the island's scenery and gentle pace of life were always in his blood, as seen in his works.

Self-Portrait, *a watercolour by Robert Harris.*

Threshing Buckwheat

Funeral at Kildare Cape

Summerside, P.E.I.

bridges would be great. Trade would be increased. Every farmer and merchant would be benefitted. Profitable employment would be given to thousands of labourers. It is impossible to overstate the advantages of a railroad. Railroads are a necessity in every country. Let us have one in Prince Edward Island where it can be constructed at a very cheap rate and where it is so much required. The Islander, *Nov. 18, 1870*

So the government promises to build a line from Georgetown to Cascumpeque Bay in three years, with branches to Souris and Tignish over the following two years. In April 1871, thousands of railway enthusiasts hold a joyous torchlight parade in Charlottetown. But there are many dissenters, especially in the country districts. Waterfront wharves are everywhere; why bother with a railway? How will turnips and potatoes travel undamaged in those jolting railway cars? What will those smoking clanging monsters do to the peace of rural countryside? Can Prince Edward Island afford the cost? But the pro-railway faction wins out. Tenders are called and a contract awarded to Messrs. Schreiber and Burpee; construction price not to exceed £5,000 a mile. Down goes the three-foot-six-inch-gauge track.

cradled in rascality

And suddenly Paradise is torn with argument. The government has neglected to specify the exact route and mileage, and the railway is taking a snakelike course. Legislators are offered bribes to bring the line through the home towns of lobbyists, and there are charges of political patronage. The Legislature is rocked with unprecedented name-calling debate. Member David Laird, editor of the *Patriot* and an anti-railway man, says the bill was "born in corruption and cradled in rascality." Premier J.C. Pope wonders aloud if a certain Opposition member is "fiend or human."

Although the soft-wood ships of P.E.I. were known on the seven seas, by 1879 iron-hulled steamers connected the tiny paradise with the great ports of the world.

**David Laird
An Islander Makes Good**

In 1857, twenty-four-year-old David Laird founded the Charlottetown *Patriot,* an ideal platform for his entry into provincial politics. Like many other Islanders, he first opposed Confederation. But even he made his peace with Canada and rather suddenly appeared in Mackenzie's Cabinet as minister of the interior. Later in the decade, he served as lieutenant-governor of the North-West Territories, negotiating the seventh treaty with the Western Indians, a long way from home.

In the end, Pope's government falls, but Premier Haythorne and his new government fare no better. They arrange with the contractors to start the branch lines immediately, hoping to hold the angry country voters at bay. But the total railway debt, in terms of Canadian currency, is already $3.25 million, or around $35 an Islander. Legislators, one and all, know they have a white elephant on their hands now. So do the people when they subsequently hear they must pay heavy taxes or join Canada. Suddenly Canada looks very good to the people of Paradise. As a pro-Confederationist has earlier remarked to Sir John A. Macdonald, "Their pockets are far more sensitive than their understanding."

There is reason to suspect that wily Sir John has hastened their understanding. In the autumn of 1872 the Island, in grave financial straits, sends its leading bank president to England to sell government debentures. He is told the bonds will sell only if Prince Edward Island joins Confederation. Obviously the Canadian government and Mother England are in cahoots. As J.C. Pope grumbles, "Influences have been brought to bear on our paper!"

business is business

Premier Haythorne goes to Ottawa, strikes a deal, comes home to call an election so that the people may express their opinion – but loses to Pope who promises, and later negotiates, a better deal with Canada. Islanders love a bargain.

By 1873 the Legislature approves Confederation with only two dissenters. One of them, A.E.C. Holland, says mournfully, "We have sold our noble little ship, and now she stands stripped of all the glory with which for a hundred years she was adorned." A number of Islanders share his sentiment, but business is business. Canada provides an advance of $800,000 to the government to buy land from proprietors and put an end to the ancient tenant system; plus a cash sum equal to $50 per person; plus new efficient steamer and telegraph service from the mainland. Best of all, Canada is taking over the two hundred miles of that infernal railway.

won at last

Even so, there is an element of gloom when the fatal hour arrives.

On Tuesday, July 1, whether for weal or woe, Prince Edward Island became a province of the Dominion of Canada. . . . But among the people who thronged the streets there was no enthusiasm. A few minutes before twelve, Mr. Sherriff Watson stepped forward on the balcony of the Colonial Building and read the union proclamation. . . . The audience within hearing consisted of three persons and even they did not appear to be very attentive.

The Patriot, *July 3, 1873*

Less than three weeks later, though, the practical Islanders have rationalized everything. When Governor General Dufferin arrives on a state visit, he passes under an archway marked LONG COURTED, WON AT LAST. Later Dufferin tells a friend that Islanders seem to feel "it is the Dominion that has been annexed to Prince Edward Island." Being a gentleman and a diplomat, he does not dispute their interpretation.

The Islanders settle down to a period of unbroken prosperity, (sweetened by the fact that the railway within ten years has lost $622,000 and Canada is stuck for it), and they live happily ever after. Or at least until the next intrusion on Paradise, thirty years later, when the Islanders rise up again – this time to ban the motorcar.

Mrs. Winslow's Soothing Syrup, an innocent brand of "gripe water" for baby's teething.

Dr. Morse's Quackery

Colourful trade cards extol the mythical powers of myriad nostrums to a nation that was skeptical of proven scientific advances such as smallpox vaccinations. If truth be told, some age-old home remedies did contain effective drugs since refined by medical science. Others contained 100-proof alcohol.

As patent medicines replaced home remedies, advertising became a "cat and mouse" business.

"Indian" recipe root pills promised healthier digestion.

Liniments, Balsams and Bitters

Rosy-cheeked children bubbling with health were the ideal presented by patent medicine vendors. In an era of high infant mortality, anxious parents administered a variety of vile remedies with the conviction that the more bitter the taste, the better the cure!

"Poor sick Tom" got Dr. Sey's for his case of feline indigestion.

To relieve chest colds and coughs, a little cherry-flavoured alcohol.

There were two ways of dealing with a toothache: a home-made ice pack or the "dentist's" pliers.

Hair Promoter - startling treatment for the cat.

Bitters restored domestic tranquility.

Worms were a common childhood disease.

A campaign to drive out depression.

CHAPTER SEVEN

A State of Grace

See Quebec and live for ever! Eternity would be too short to weary me of this lovely scene.

The Golden Dog, William Kirby, 1877

On the afternoon of September 2, 1875, a melancholy procession led by two black horses drawing a flag-draped coffin wended along a Montreal dirt road to Côte des Neiges cemetery. After six uneasy years in Protestant ground, the body of Joseph Guibord, a local printer, was finally going to its proper rest in Roman Catholic turf.

Or was it? As the funeral cortège approached the cemetery gates, a rowdy crowd of nearly a thousand – many of them drunk – barred the way, hurling stones, brandishing clubs and shouting "God damn Guibord!" and "Take the cursed Guibord away!" The mourners and carriages hesitated, retreated and returned the corpse to its vault in Mount Royal cemetery. Poor Guibord – an unwitting pawn in the most bizarre and bitter religious-political struggle of the day – was not yet to rest in peace.

In life, Guibord had been, said the *Canadian Illustrated News,* "a man of irreproachable morals, of the steadiest habits, of rigid honesty and altogether a model workman." Even his strong craggy face, framed in grey-flecked hair, seemed to attest to his probity. Two deep worry-lines furrowed his forehead, bespeaking a serious man

who shunned frivolity in all its insidious forms. The worry-lines would have been deeper still if Guibord could have foreseen his after-life. In death he became a *cause célèbre,* for he died in November 1869, on the eve of a decade of religious furore.

Most Canadians of the seventies firmly held to the doctrines (and biases) of one or another stern religion. For Protestant or Catholic and all other believers, the church was not only a religious centre but a social centre. Newspapers regularly covered the Sunday sermons and reported them as the news of Monday's edition. Canadians took their religion seriously and made little effort to tolerate or understand any one else's faith. The Orangemen, historically linked to Irish Protestantism, were convinced that all Catholics were agents of the devil. Staunch Catholics believed without question that their clergy had a direct pipeline to the Almighty. The Vatican Council's promulgation in 1870 of the doctrine of papal infallibility had strengthened this belief. As Bishop Ignace Bourget of Montreal advised his flock in a private circular of 1876, "Let us each say in his heart, 'I hear my curé, my curé hears the bishop, the bishop hears the Pope and the Pope hears Our Lord Jesus Christ.'"

The Catholic Church itself, particularly in Quebec, was torn with religious and political dissension. Its more conservative clergy believed

Dressed in the sheepskin and bearing the banner of Quebec's patron saint, this youngster also sports a maple leaf for the annual parade.

Opposite page: Habitant revellers crowd the verandah in Cornelius Kreighoff's 1871 painting of J.B. Jolifou's country inn.

THE UNQUIET GRAVE

The six-year legal battle fought by Doutre (right) to have the corpse of excommunicated Institiut member Guibord (left) buried in consecrated ground was won in 1875. The solid stone coffin (below) ensured that the body could not be removed by irate Catholics.

that the church's moral law had supremacy over civil law. But other Catholics, equally strong in their religious convictions, believed that the laws of "the state" should prevail over the church. This group included many young intellectuals who, influenced by the European philosophies of liberalism and socialism, formed the nucleus of the provincial Liberals or *Rouges*. Conservative bishops equated the Liberalism of the Rouges with the anti-clerical liberalism of Europe and tended to give votive political support to the Conservative *Bleus*. What they commonly saw as a "simple struggle between good and evil" verged perilously on an attempt to limit political freedom in Quebec. The Guibord affair was this struggle in microcosm.

the Institut Canadien

Joseph Guibord had been, in life, a member and vice-president of the Institut Canadien. Organized in the 1840s, the Institut provided clubs and reading rooms that became discussion centres for Rouge philosophies. The Institut in Montreal was frequently condemned by Bishop Bourget who, in 1869, convinced Rome to ban the group for harbouring prohibited books and doctrines. Any who refused to renounce their membership were denied the sacraments of the Church. Guibord had refused and, when he died, the bishop refused permission for a Catholic burial.

While he lay in unconsecrated ground, his wife Henriette, with lawyer Joseph Doutre and some other Institut friends took the case to court. An 1870 judgement found for the widow and ordered the cemetery to pay costs. An appeal court reversed the judgement, and was upheld by the Court of Queen's Bench. Meanwhile Henriette died and was peaceably buried in Côte des Neiges cemetery. Her husband remained banished among the Protestants.

Doutre stubbornly carried the case to England.

There in November 1874, the highest court in the Empire ruled that the Catholic parish must bury Guibord and pay the costs, now totalling $6,000. Jubilant, Doutre and his friends pressed their luck and demanded a religious ceremony for the second burial. It was more than the bishop and his followers could swallow. So, on the September afternoon in 1875, Guibord was rejected at the very brink of his Catholic grave.

Then Governor General Dufferin quietly let it be known that the Queen's law must prevail. The mayor of Montreal added his influence. Bishop Bourget reluctantly issued a circular instructing his people to stay calm. On November 16 with an escort of police and militia Guibord's coffin, "looking somewhat dilapidated," returned yet again to Côte des Neiges. As cold rain drizzled down on snow-patched mud, the coffin settled into the family plot atop Madame Guibord's, and was encased in cement mixed with scraps of metal to discourage vandalism.

A hostile crowd hovered nearby. The mayor ordered police to stand guard until the cement hardened. Even so, Bishop Bourget had the last word: Guibord's grave would forever be deemed unconsecrated ground. His wife a few inches beneath him remained in a state of grace.

tranquil and charming

How incongruous this holy warfare all seemed in a province so gentle to the eye. Let us step back in time, through the writing of George Monro Grant, into a Quebec as tranquil and charming as a Krieghoff painting. . . .

Quebec City this day is cloaked in rosy morning mists astride its mass of rock. Its rough-hewn plank sidewalks stagger down the contours of its slopes. We feast our eyes on "narrow crooked lanes that do duty for streets, the grimy weather-beaten walls and narrow windows on either side, the steep-roofed antique French houses, the corkscrew ascent toward the upper town, the rugged pavement over which the wheels of the calèche rattle noisily." Beyond the docks "heaped high with fragrant wood," the St. Lawrence is glutted with shipping: three-masters, stern-wheelers, bateaux with great square sails, British men-of-war with seamen rigged out in flat straw hats and blue jackets with brass buttons.

We follow the river-highway with its narrow farms strung out on either bank. Long ago these *terres* were three arpents wide by 30 deep (an arpent is 191 feet). Now, subdivided to accommodate growing families, there seem to be more wooden fences than fields.

The countryside is all white cottages with roofs in throbbing primary colors, riots of flowers in front and ribbons of ground behind. Whole families toil in the flax and hay fields, the men red-capped, the women in blue shirts and voluminous hats. Yoked oxen tug the ploughs, and sturdy black dogs haul carts of wood and milk.

the Church is law

We pause to sip clear icy water trickling down a hillside from a hidden spring. A shy dark-eyed child is sent from a nearby house to ask, "Monsieur will not by preference have some milk?" We visit the home of a *gros habitant,* a well-to-do farmer – a long one-storey cottage "prim with whitewash," chimney rising on the outer wall and a gallery in front where the man may rest of an evening with his evil-smelling pipe. The shutters will be closed at night, from generations of habit, harking back to times when Iroquois lurked in the woods. Now there are no dangers, just hard work by day, supper and a song or two at night and, always, the tight embrace of family and church.

The Church's presence is everywhere: in the

**Archbishop Taschereau
First Canadian Cardinal**

Elzéar Alexandre Taschereau, born in 1820, was educated at the Quebec Seminary, where he spent almost 30 years as a professor and as Superior. In 1871, as Archbishop of Quebec, he united with other bishops on the Guibord affair, but later led the group that forbade priests to influence parishioners on political matters. At the age of 76, he became the first Canadian to be consecrated a Cardinal of the Catholic Church.

Keeping the Sabbath Holy

In a strongly religious age, almost all the three and a half million Canadians faithfully observed the Sabbath. Indeed one day's rest in seven was welcome relief from the tedium of work. But whether Protestant, Catholic or Jewish, the place of worship also served as social centre of a religious community.

The Sabbath as a day of rest and devotions was strictly observed in backwoods Canada.

These altar boys were caught taking an unauthorized sip of the wine prepared for a service of communion.

L'Opinion Publique *published in 1874 this representation of a Yom Kippur service, held in one of the two synagogues in Montreal, home of Canada's largest Jewish community.*

Four provincial organizations united in 1875 as the Presbyterian Church in Canada. Each delegate's photograph was taken individually in a preplanned pose, mounted in the "composite" arrangement above, and rephotographed.

Public Opinion, Québec

The success of his *Canadian Illustrated News* in 1869 encouraged publisher George Desbarats to launch a French-language counterpart in January 1870. *L'Opinion Publique's* editors did not rely only on translation of the English magazine's articles, but wrote original editorials and published French and Québecois authors.

The weekly magazine had a 14-year life span, like its sister publication.

Artists for the illustrated journals of the period had to work quickly.

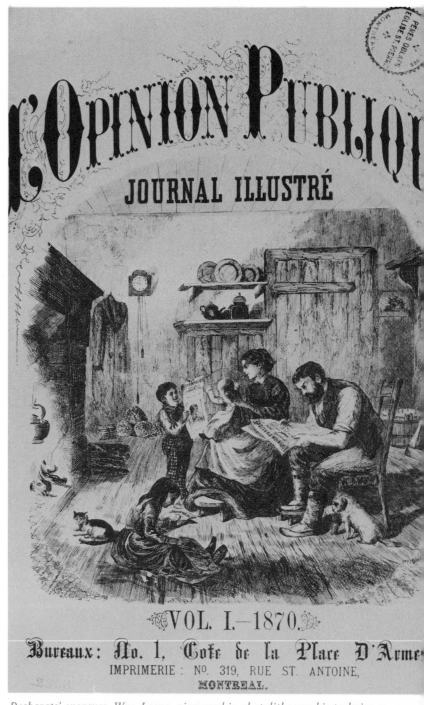

Desbarats' engraver, Wm. Leggo, pioneered in photolithographic techniques.

black cassocks whispering along the boardwalks of Quebec City, in shimmering spires and wayside chapels, and in village names that cry out the faith: Ile Jésus, Ste. Croix, L'Epiphanie, Notre-Dame-des-Anges. For these countryfolk, who are the backbone of Quebec, the Church is the centre of life. The Church is *law*. . . .

the blue banner of the Pope

The holy war shook Quebec to its roots. In 1871 a group of conservative churchmen laid down rules for voting: in any electoral contest "between a Conservative of any shade whatever and an adept of the Liberal school, our active sympathies will be given to the former." In two federal by-elections of 1876 the fight moved openly into the electorate. Curés warned their parishioners that a Liberal vote involved mortal sin, and one flatly stated that the Conservatives carried the blue banner of the Pope. It followed that the loyal Catholic was to vote Bleu, the colour of heaven, not Rouge, the colour of the fires of hell.

A moderate Liberal, Laurent-Olivier David, after seeing his publication *Bien Public* banned in one parish after another, bitterly gave up that paper. "The profession of politics has become intolerable in this country," he said. "In the name of religion we have seen destruction fall upon the political careers of sincere and honest men whose religious convictions have never been questioned."

While this battle raged within the church, the Quebec Catholics were locked in an age-old tussle with the Loyal Orange Order. By the mid-seventies the 200,000 Orangemen in Canada, mostly in Ontario, represented thirty percent of all the country's Protestant males over twenty-one. They hated Catholics so much that any man who married one was instantly expelled from the Order. Louis Riel's execution of Orangeman Thomas

Scott in Manitoba still gnawed at their souls. Another killing, on July 12, 1877, brought all the passions surging to the surface.

In Montreal that day, Orangemen from both provinces paraded in full regalia, as every year, to honour King William of Orange's victory over the Catholic King James II in 1690. About noon a threatening crowd gathered around the Orange Hall on St. James Street. Soon two women, one wearing the orange lily, got into a fight. A man who tried to intervene was badly roughed up. Orangeman Thomas Hackett, a 20-year-old clerk on his way home from church, got into the fracas, allegedly pulled a gun and was shot through the head and throat.

the orange lily

Ontario was enraged. Hackett, said the Toronto *Telegram,* was "a quiet young man of strictly temperate habits." Twelve hundred Ontario Orangemen poured into Montreal under military protection for Hackett's funeral four days later. The grand master of Kingston said ominously, "We have come to protect the Orangemen of Montreal on this occasion and woe betide this city if we have to come again."

A year later on July 12, Montreal was a powder keg, but strict measures and common sense prevailed. Many Ontario Orangemen stayed home. Parliament had passed the Crimes of Violence Prevention Act, forbidding the carrying of dangerous weapons. Montreal police promptly arrested several Orange leaders for violation of the Act and kept the rank and file pinned down in the Orange Hall. A restive crowd of Irish and French, prowling the streets in search of trouble, eventually went home disappointed.

There were other signs that Quebec's strife was easing. Young Wilfrid Laurier, a vice-president of the Institut Canadien before Guibord, won a seat

Vitriolic denunciations of political candidates were common. M. Paquet was nevertheless reelected and became provincial secretary in 1879.

**Wilfrid Laurier
A Young Liberal**

Wilfrid Laurier, born in St. Lin in 1841 showed his inclination to Liberalism by joining a legal firm affiliated with the Parti Rouge, and becoming a vice-president of the Institut Canadien. In spite of poor health, he was active in politics, in the provincial legislature in 1871 and in the federal House in 1874. By the end of the decade he had emerged as the most promising French Canadian Liberal, a future prime minister.

in the provincial legislature in 1871, despite open harassment from the clergy. By 1874 he had a federal seat in Mackenzie's new Liberal government. Laurier made no secret of his distaste for the religious-political turmoil in his native province. On June 26, 1877, he arose before the Club Canadien in Quebec City – tall, thin and arrow straight, his aquiline face pale but composed, his voice sonorous and deliberate – and delivered the speech of a lifetime:

We have no absolute rights. The rights of each man in our state of society end precisely at the point where they encroach upon the rights of others. The right of interference in politics ends at the point where it encroaches upon the elector's independence. The constitution of the country rests upon the freely expressed wish of each elector. It intends that each elector shall cast his vote freely and willingly as he deems best. . . .

I flatter myself that I have some sincere friends among [the clergy] and to them I can and do say: see if there is under the sun a country where the Catholic Church is freer or more privileged than it is here. Why then should you, by claiming rights incompatible with our state of society, expose this country to agitations of which it is impossible to foresee the consequences?

It was Laurier's finest hour, and it raised him

from obscure backbencher to national statesman. Supporting sentiment was rising all around him. Archbishop Taschereau had issued a pastoral letter, putting both political parties on equal footing and urging electors to calmly assess their merits. Next the Superior Court of Quebec annulled a by-election wherein two curés had threatened to withhold the sacraments from Catholics who voted for Liberals. Then the Vatican itself sent an Irish bishop to Quebec to sort out the quarrels. From his mission came a joint pastoral letter that distinguished between liberalism in the Catholic Church (of which the Vatican disapproved) and Liberalism in party politics. An accompanying circular to the clergy spelled out the new order: they were expressly forbidden to teach "from the pulpit or anywhere else that it is a sin to vote for any particular candidate or party; even more is it forbidden that you will refuse the sacraments for this cause."

French-Canadian nationalism would simmer and bubble on through the years. Religious trouble would flare again. But the principle of separate religious and political freedoms was firmly established. A future French-Canadian prime minister – the nation's first – had emerged. Canada's two solitudes were inching their way toward an understanding. And perhaps Joseph Guibord, in death, had contributed more than he could have dreamed of in his lifetime.

A Canadian Dynasty

The great Massey manufacturing dynasty had its beginnings in tiny Cobourg, Upper Canada, where Daniel Massey established a small foundry. By 1870 his eldest son, Hart, had shaped it into the Massey Manufacturing Co., and the next two decades saw the phenomenal growth of the firm culminating in the 1891 merger with the Harris Co. Much of the family fortune was spent on philanthropic projects to commemorate various Masseys — Charles, Fred Victor, Lillian and Hart himself. But two of Hart Massey's grandsons vastly enlarged the family's reputation — Vincent, who became the first Canadian-born governor general, and Raymond, renowned star of stage and film.

Daniel Massey (1798-1856) implement manufacturer, father of eleven children, the eldest being . . .

Hart Massey (1823-1896) built up the family's small manufacturing firm; father of five sons.

Chester Massey (1850-1926) Hart's second son in charge of the Massey Foundation; father of Vincent and Raymond.

Walter Massey (1858-1901) Hart's third son, head of advertising in the eighties; began Massey's Illustrated.

No Equal or No Sale

The Massey skill lay in recognizing good quality machinery, putting it together and marketing it. The firm achieved its medals not for machines of its own invention but for the good performance of the implements that it manufactured from purchased patents.

An 1879 ad for this Massey Harvester listed a dozen "points of excellence."

Success at the Paris exposition in 1867 led to Massey's first exports and a string of medals at both national and international exhibitions.

One satisfied user of this Sharp's Rake suggested Massey sell it on the terms "No Equal or no pay."

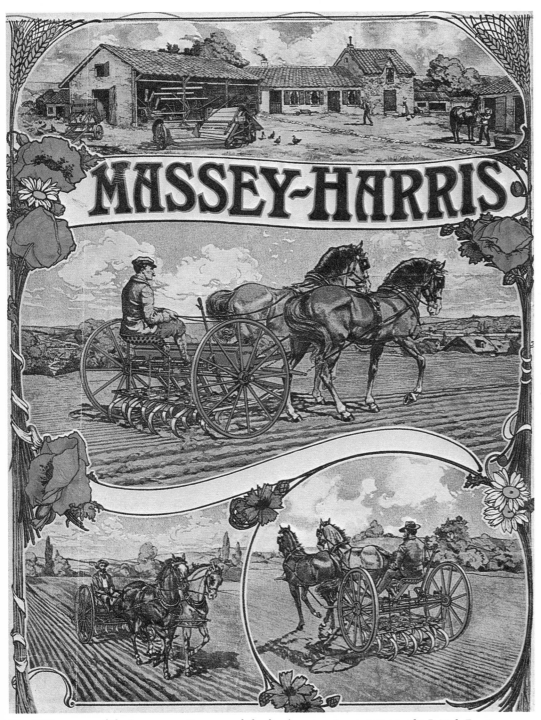

The 1891 merger of the two companies ensured the firm's pre-eminent status in the British Empire.

Patriotic and religious themes were interwoven on a linen pillowcase for wives of prospective buyers.

Massey acquired the Toronto Binder Company in '81.

CHAPTER EIGHT

Moving into the Big Time

All of our Machines and Implements are made of the best material and in the best manner.

Advertisement of the Massey Manufacturing Co., 1878

It was such an excellent machine that farmer F.W. Whelihan of Thornhill Place, Ontario, felt obliged to squander a three-cent stamp to tell the manufacturer so. On August 24, 1877, he put quill to paper and addressed the Massey Manufacturing Company of Newcastle, Ontario:

Gentlemen: I purchased one of your Sharp's Horse Rakes from your agent. I am very much pleased with it. A boy six years old, with a pony, raked 45 acres of hay and about 30 acres of stubble, and the little fellow feels proud of his pony and Sulky Rake.

The Masseys were very fast men with a testimonial and this one made page one of their 1878 catalogue. There, in woodcut illustration, was the Little Fellow, almost lost in his enormous felt hat and the curved metal seat of the rake, but working along manfully, his perky black horse stepping firmly toward distant hills and an idyllic farmhouse: the Good Canadian Life.

The Masseys did tend to idealize that life, but this was a good period for them and for Canadian agriculture. During it, the Massey company took the decisive step from small-town shop to big-city factory, a move that would make it the most famous name in Canadian farm machinery.

Farming in progressive Ontario was well on its way to mechanization. Farmers were eager for the new machinery and Massey made the best. "How beautifully and easily the machine passes through the hard places!" exclaimed a Massey advertisement for a mower-reaper. "And how perfect and uniform is all the work done!" Ease and perfection – those were the new watchwords of agriculture.

Eighty percent of the country's half million adult males worked on farms, mostly as owners of properties of fifty to two hundred acres. They kept over eight hundred thousand horses, three million sheep and two and a half million cattle. In an average year they produced about seventeen million bushels of wheat, forty-two million of oats, forty-seven million of potatoes, twenty-four million of turnips, and lesser amounts of barley, peas, corn, buckwheat, hay, wool and honey. The farmer supported himself and fed the nation. He was one of its most envied persons, not for his manners nor his wealth (the rich farmer was in the minority) but for his independence. He was his own man, the very spirit of this new Canada.

If he sought a gentle almost biblical kind of existence he found it among the fields of hay, barley, oats, maize, buckwheat, hemp and flax of rural Quebec. Good land could be rented near Montreal for $3 an acre, or purchased outright for

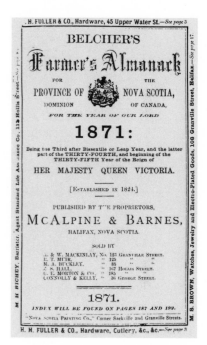

Belcher's Almanack, one of at least 20 almanacs published in Nova Scotia, went far beyond astronomy and astrology to provide advice and information to farmers.

Opposite page: Massey acquired the patents to produce Sharp's Rake in 1875 and within four years the firm had made and sold 7,500 units.

93

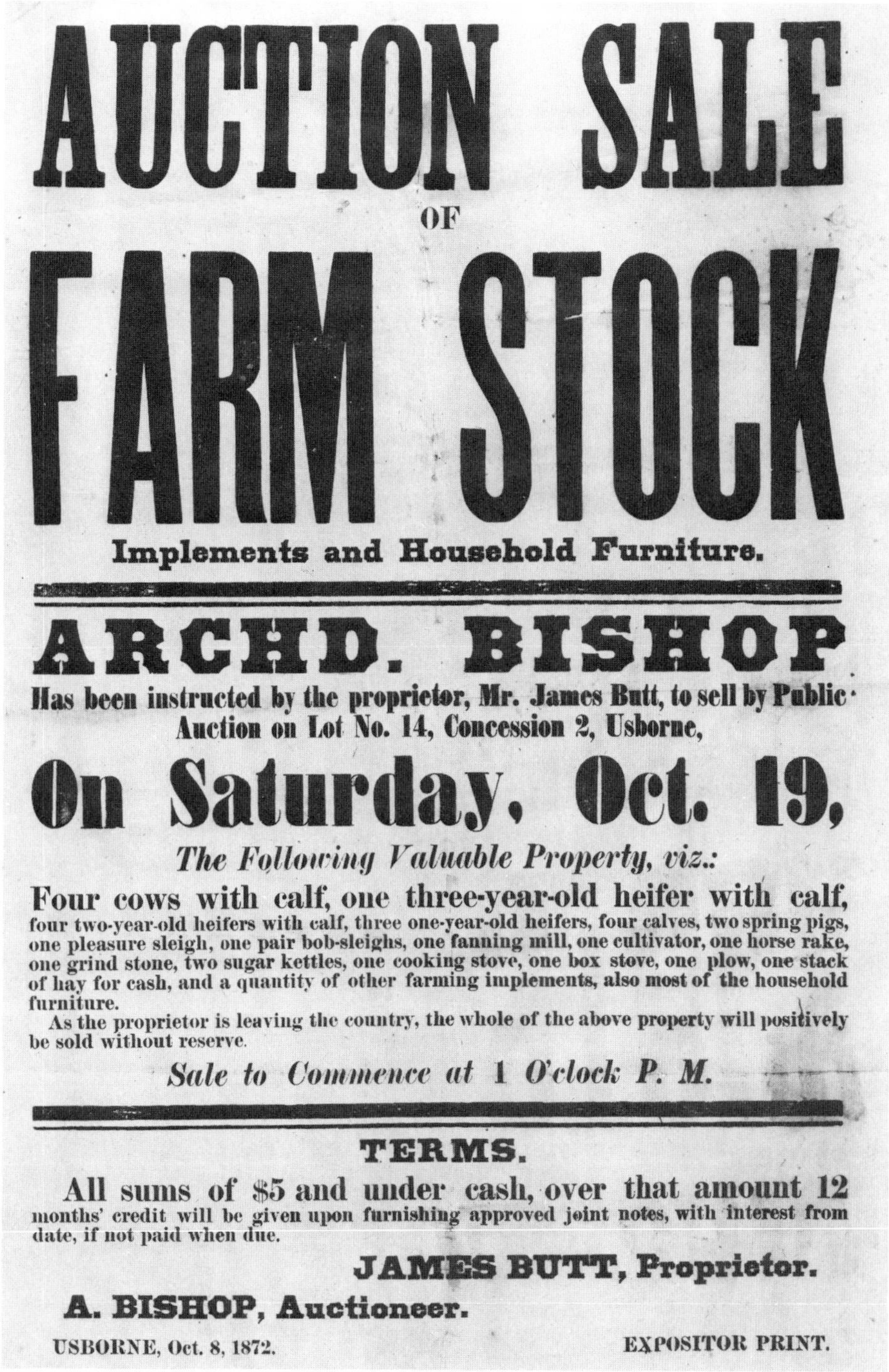

AUCTION SALE
OF
FARM STOCK

Implements and Household Furniture.

ARCHD. BISHOP

Has been instructed by the proprietor, Mr. James Butt, to sell by Public
Auction on Lot No. 14, Concession 2, Usborne,

On Saturday, Oct. 19,

The Following Valuable Property, viz.:

Four cows with calf, one three-year-old heifer with calf,
four two-year-old heifers with calf, three one-year-old heifers, four calves, two spring pigs,
one pleasure sleigh, one pair bob-sleighs, one fanning mill, one cultivator, one horse rake,
one grind stone, two sugar kettles, one cooking stove, one box stove, one plow, one stack
of hay for cash, and a quantity of other farming implements, also most of the household
furniture.

As the proprietor is leaving the country, the whole of the above property will positively
be sold without reserve.

Sale to Commence at 1 O'clock P. M.

TERMS.

All sums of $5 and under cash, over that amount 12
months' credit will be given upon furnishing approved joint notes, with interest from
date, if not paid when due.

JAMES BUTT, Proprietor.
A. BISHOP, Auctioneer.

USBORNE, Oct. 8, 1872.　　　　　　　　　　EXPOSITOR PRINT.

$50. Habitants of the late seventies still used scythes, sickles, homemade ploughs and, for harrows, "a lot of brushwood fastened to a beam." Mechanized farming had not found its way to Quebec, but life amid the emerald green fields and the distant toll of village church bells was full of simple satisfactions. "Threshing is still done by flails and strong arms," wrote George Monro Grant, at the end of the decade. "Once in a while you may hear the rattle of a treadmill where the little black pony tramps away as sleepily and contentedly as his master sits on a fence rail smoking."

a trickle of immigrants

For the ultimate in pioneering a man rattled out to Minnesota six days and $25 away by train (late in the decade the railway went right on to Winnipeg), rode north by wagon or Red River paddle-wheeler and tried his luck in Manitoba. The Dominion Lands Act of 1872 offered him a quarter-section (160 acres) of land for only a $10 fee, on condition that he reside on it and work it for three years. If he met his obligations on that first quarter-section, it was his and he could pre-empt a second quarter-section.

The trickle of immigrants turned into a tide: eager young men from Ontario where the best land was already gone, Icelanders retreating from a volcanic eruption that had covered hundreds of square miles of their homeland with pumice, thousands of German-speaking Mennonites from the Ukraine. The land was free of pesky trees; the air was dry and tangy as vintage champagne. If a settler could scrape up $500, he bought a yoke of oxen, a cow, a wagon, plough, harrow, cookstove, simple furniture and a year's provisions for a family. From then on it was a glorious gamble between him, the grasshoppers, drought, prairie fires and rich virgin earth.

Manufacturers demonstrated new lines of farm machinery and farmers matched their own and their team's skills at ploughing competitions.

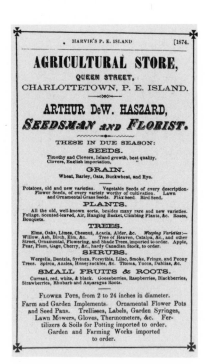

Using store-bought seed reduced the "hazards" of the growing season for customers of this agricultural store in the garden province.

Even here science was lending a hand. When grasshoppers stripped the fields bare in 1875, Red River farmers had to buy new seed-grain and selected Red Fife, a hard, rust-resistant strain of spring wheat developed by David Fife, a Scot from Peterborough, Ontario. It was already preferred in central Canada and the northern states for the excellent flour produced by new milling methods. Now, in the glorious black loam of Manitoba, Red Fife performed magic. The crop of 1876 matured two weeks ahead of the old Red River variety, with twenty-five bushels to the acre of plump hard grain. A Toronto seed-buyer came clamouring for 5,000 bushels – "Cash for choice wheat to export to Ontario" cried the *Manitoba Free Press* announcement – and had to content himself with 857 bushels, every kernel the local farmers could spare. By 1878 wheat had surpassed fur as Manitoba's prime product and the era of the prairie "bread basket" was born.

Ontarians, who had never seen flour so fine, were enchanted. More and more the Ontario farmer was engrossed with the science of his profession. He was into diversified production such as fruit, beef and dairy farming, even bee-keeping. He pored over such fledgling publications as the *Ontario Farmer* for tips on when and what to plant, how to fertilize with barnyard manure, how to utilize his off-season hours, or how farmer-specialists like Senator George Brown, publisher of the Toronto *Globe,* raised two crops a year on his Brantford acreage, cutting the first one green to feed his 300 Shorthorns.

The master farmer was likewise intrigued with the Ontario School of Agriculture, founded at Guelph in 1874 with two-year courses in practical

In response to the new idea that a man needed an education to farm, the Ontario School of Agriculture opened in 1874.

farming. Its standards were stiff: entrants had to pass examinations in reading, writing, arithmetic, spelling and geography. Yet within four years it had 146 students.

Little wonder that the first-class farmer lived almost as well as a Montreal railway magnate. His table was heaped with home-cured bacon and ham, beef, mutton, chicken, fruit, vegetables and an endless variety of game. Often his bank account was heaped with cash.

A case in point was a Guelph man who in 1879 had two hundred acres of choice well-fenced land, good orchard, a one-and-a-half-storey house, six horses, six cows and assorted calves, colts, ewes, lambs and steers. His year's expenses, including two hired men, a hired girl and $60 taxes, totalled $925. His net profit from grain and livestock was $1,260, more than the average city labourer

grossed in two years. He owned $800 worth of equipment – plough, rake, mower, reaper and cultivator – and closely watched the newest offerings of Canada's two hundred and fifty machinery makers. Most of them were mere blacksmiths though; the firm to really watch was Massey.

The Masseys were themselves farmers and tinkerers. Daniel, who had started the firm in 1847, was a blacksmith with a consuming curiosity for machines. His son, Hart – born in a log cabin, hauling grain at age ten, working in a lumber camp at eighteen – took over the family's little Newcastle Agricultural Works at twenty-eight. By 1870 his ferocious energy had brought it a long way from the blacksmith shop. Hart, a gaunt six-footer with a face like a pine carving, made and marketed most kinds of American-designed farm machinery: a combined reaper and mower, rakes,

"Gristing and chopping done every day, water permitting." The water-wheel mills were still operating in the 1870s; steam power had not yet won over the millers.

Hart Massey is front and centre of his machinists in this 1884 photo. Each man displays his contribution.

Come to the Fair

The Crystal Palace (above), first erected in 1858, was moved to Exhibition Park and given a new first floor for the Toronto Industrial Exhibition of 1879 (below), now the C.N.E.

feed choppers, cultivators, ploughs, stump pullers (a chain and crank device slung from a tripod) and "horsepowers." These were great stationary gadgets with iron gears and long wooden sweeps that were moved by horses plodding continuously in a circle. Through a hook-up of belts, the horsepower could drive any stationary machine.

Workmanship was what made Massey machines unique; they even worked better than their American originals. By this time every Canadian community had an annual fall fair; by the end of the seventies, Toronto's Industrial Exhibition Association erected permanent buildings for its yearly Exhibition. Every fair, along with its baking contests, needlework displays and patent medicine men had a machinery contest. Massey won prizes in Canada, France, Germany and the United States. At the Paris International Exposition of 1867 the company had taken a first grand prize and two gold medals and earned congratulations from Emperor Napoleon III himself. A few months later while a Newcastle crowd cheered and the town band blew itself red in the face, Massey shipped twenty mowers and reapers off to Germany in boxcars plastered with bunting – the first exports.

winning wild cheers

At forty-seven and slowing down on doctor's orders, Hart formed the Massey Manufacturing Company, a joint – stock firm with himself as president and his son, Charles, as vice-president and superintendent. Then he moved to Cleveland to take it easy. Charles was twenty-three, even taller than Hart, with the same famous Massey face and the same passion for work. He moved his bride into a white frame house, and for him the plant next door was a second home. He increased business by fifty percent in his first four years. One shrewd move was buying Canadian rights to the Sharp Self-Dumping Hay and Stubble Rake, an early version of the model so admired by the Little Fellow in Thornhill Place. It was an immediate hit with farmers and a consistent winner in the contests held all over the East in the seventies. These were a mixture of entertainment and advertising; manufacturers pitted their newest rake, plough, or reaper against their rivals, in the presence of judges. The one that left the cleanest stubble or neatest furrow won wild cheers from the onlookers and extravagant adjectives in the company's next advertising circulars.

moving into the big time

In 1876, with Canada deep in depression, Charles Massey grossed $100,000 and told a parliamentary committee that *his* company, at least, didn't need any more tariff protection. Part of Charles' success was his flair for showmanship. His slogan "No Equal or No Sale" appealed to every bargain-hunting farmer; anyone who didn't like a new Massey machine and could demonstrate in competition an equal or better one, got a refund. The yearly Massey catalogue glowed with testimonials and gloated at the latest contest wins over other manufacturers.

The little Newcastle plant was running at capacity. In 1878 it turned out twenty-one hundred Sharp's Rakes and the first totally Canadian reaper. This Massey Harvester was not revolutionary: it didn't, for example, bind sheaves; farmers still did that by hand. But the Harvester was the best on the market: solidly made of wrought-iron and steel and equipped with levers to tilt the cutting blade, lift the entire cutting table over rocks, and change gears for light or heavy crops. When farmers discovered that it rarely broke down – something of a novelty in machinery then – Massey was swamped with five hundred orders, more than double his planned production. By

working night and day shifts, the plant built three hundred and fifty-six by year's end.

The 1879 catalogue treated this coup with a suitable mixture of reverence and exuberance. It explained how the crop of '78 had been heavy and tangled yet "the Harvester worked its way through like a little hero, surprising everyone and delighting its purchasers." Its success "far surpassed our most sanguine expectations." A four-colour lithograph showed the little red-green-gold hero dominating a field of ripening grain with one of those idealized farmhouses in the background, dreamlike and delicate as a Monet print. The catalogue added that Massey would make up to a thousand Harvesters in 1879. And customers should address all future correspondence to Toronto.

For Massey was moving into the big time. By 1880 a new factory occupied six acres on Toronto's King Street, three storeys of red brick with gaslight and automatic fire sprinklers. Hart, realizing that this sprawling enterprise was more of a bite than even Charles could chew alone, came home to help. From then on, the Masseys never looked back.

from farm to city

Neither, in a sense, did Canadian agriculture. Farming steadily became more professional and more profitable. Yet before the decade ended, the monthly magazine, *Ontario Farmer,* reported a strange and melancholy trend: farm boys in increasing numbers were leaving home for the city. "It may well be considered a public, nay a national calamity," said the magazine. What could be done about it? The *Ontario Farmer* could only lamely suggest that farm parents try to make rural life more appealing to their sons. But it added prophetically, "The trend will probably continue as long as human occupations are as varied and numerous as they now are."

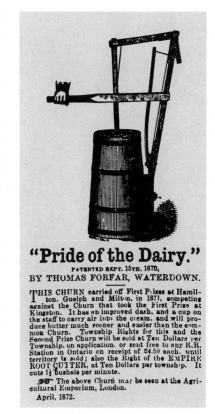

"Pride of the Dairy."
PATENTED SEPT. 15TH, 1870,
BY THOMAS FORFAR, WATERDOWN.

THIS CHURN carried off First Prizes at Hamilton, Guelph and Milton, in 1871, competing against the Churn that took the First Prize at Kingston. It has an improved dash, and a cup on the staff to carry air into the cream, and will produce butter much sooner and easier than the common Churn. Township Rights for this and the Second Prize Churn will be sold at Ten Dollars per Township, on application, or sent free to any R.R. Station in Ontario on receipt of $4.50 each, until territory is sold; also the Right of the EMPIRE ROOT CUTTER, at Ten Dollars per township. It cuts 1½ bushels per minute.

☞ The above Churn may be seen at the Agricultural Emporium, London.

April, 1872.

In the decade when the cream separator was invented, Canadian farmers were churning butter both for domestic use and for export.

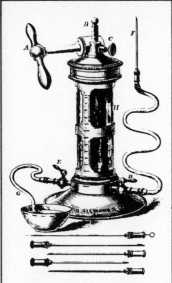

Dieulafoy's Aspirator

Cheatham's Ether
Inhaler

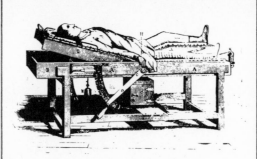

Morgan's Fracture Bed

Leg Splint (note fig leaf)

Ear Trumpet

Pravaz's Hypodermic Syringe

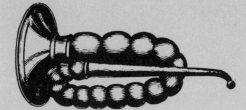

Canvas Straight Jacket
with Lock

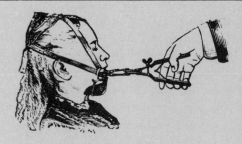

The Gradual Cure For Lockjaw

Sayres' Improved
Clubfoot Shoe

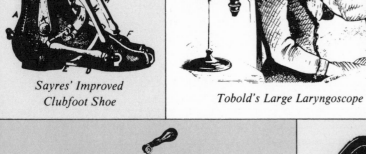

Tobold's Large Laryngoscope

Heine's Saw

Mathieu's Tonsilotome

Dentist's Leather Instrument Pouch

Graefe's Circular Saw   Brace Trepan

Bullet Forceps

CHAPTER NINE

The Unfortunate Case of Bill Harris

Cure for Ague: Four ounces galangal root in a quart of gin, steeped . . . take often.

The Canadian Home Cook Book, 1877

The unfortunate case of Bill Harris, reduced to its basic facts, came down to this: he died of a broken thigh after the best available treatment in one of Canada's finest hospitals – and in 1870 this was in no way unusual. On November 14, the 23-year-old Montreal labourer was unloading molasses from a wagon and caught the full weight of a falling hogshead in his lap. They carried him into Montreal General, a four-storey hospital of 150 beds, staffed by some of Canada's best doctors (soon to include the brilliant William Osler). Routine procedure was to tie leather splints and cotton batting immediately around the fracture, apply a wooden splint from chest to toe and hope the bones would knit.

For a while, Harris seemed reasonably comfortable and didn't complain. But on the third day his physician noted that the leg was "cold, partly insensible and with bluish-black discolouration." On the sixth it was "looking bad." There were no antibiotics. Indeed, the fact that the doctors next prescribed a wash of a 1 to 20 carbolic solution showed they were in the forefront of medical science. Only six years before, Pasteur had discovered unseen living organisms in the air; only a year

after that, Lister had introduced carbolic solutions, hoping to kill such organisms and reduce putrefaction of wounds.

Harris' pulse was 128 by the fourth day. On the ninth day, the doctors decided to amputate. It was a slim chance – two-thirds of thigh amputees died after surgery – but the only one. Harris was carried to a narrow wooden table in the operating room. There were no sanitary preparations. Lister's idea of spraying the room with carbolic solution before surgery and his overall theory of antisepsis (total cleanliness and sterilization) were just evolving. It was still common for a surgeon to mop his own perspiring forehead or pick a fallen instrument from the floor during an operation.

A junior assistant applied chloroform with a cloth compress to Harris' nose. Although the more dangerous chloroform killed one patient in every 2,800 compared to ether's one in 23,000, most Canadian doctors used it anyway because it was quicker, with less disagreeable after-effects. The surgeon slipped on a frock-coat – no mask, gloves or gown – and, with a forged-steel unplated knife, made two deft angular cuts around the middle third of the thigh. Then, while his assistant held back the flaps that would later be folded over the stump, he bared the bone and cut through with a kind of hacksaw. He tied the arteries with silk, clamped a vein with a metal pin, cleaned the wound with carbolic solution and closed it with

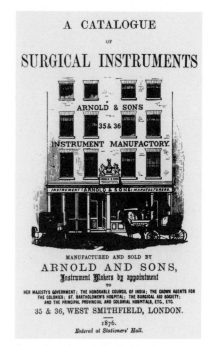

A CATALOGUE OF SURGICAL INSTRUMENTS

ARNOLD & SONS

35 & 36

INSTRUMENT MANUFACTORY.

MANUFACTURED AND SOLD BY
ARNOLD AND SONS,
Instrument Makers by appointment
TO
HER MAJESTY'S GOVERNMENT; THE HONORABLE COUNCIL OF INDIA; THE CROWN AGENTS FOR THE COLONIES; ST. BARTHOLOMEW'S HOSPITAL; THE SURGICAL AID SOCIETY; AND THE PRINCIPAL PROVINCIAL AND COLONIAL HOSPITALS, ETC. ETC.

35 & 36, WEST SMITHFIELD, LONDON.
1876.
Entered at Stationers' Hall.

Canadian doctors looked to British or American catalogues for their complement of medical equipment.

Opposite page: The items illustrated here were taken from catalogues of medical instruments available to doctors in the age of innocence.

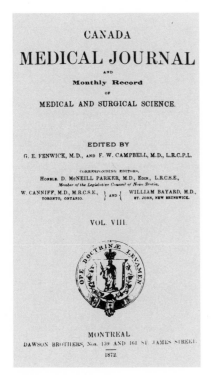

CANADA

MEDICAL JOURNAL

AND

Monthly Record

OF

MEDICAL AND SURGICAL SCIENCE.

EDITED BY

G. E. FENWICK, M.D., AND F. W. CAMPBELL, M.D., L.R.C.P.L.

CORRESPONDING EDITORS.

HONBLE. D. McNEILL PARKER, M.D., EDIN., L.R.C.S.E.,
Member of the Legislative Council of Nova Scotia,

W. CANNIFF, M.D., M.R.C.S.E., } AND { WILLIAM BAYARD, M.D.,
TORONTO, ONTARIO.   ST. JOHN, NEW BRUNSWICK.

VOL. VIII.

MONTREAL
DAWSON BROTHERS, Nos. 159 AND 161 ST. JAMES STREET.
1872.

Articles in the pages of Canada
Medical Journal *expressed doctors'*
concerns with the ravages of diseases
such as scarlet fever, whooping
cough and consumption.

silver wire. (Catgut, another Lister idea, was known but not yet widely adopted). He shed his blood-soaked coat, a porter mopped up the mess and Harris was returned to his ward.

At first he seemed to be doing well: "Stump easy. Eating well. Pulse 100. Gave him half-grain of morphia in solution which enabled him to sleep." The next day he tossed deliriously and lost the clamp on his vein "which was found on the floor." (Harris was lucky to have a single bed. More primitive hospitals considered *two* patients to a bed in a public ward proper and even kind.) The surgeon removed alternate sutures to ease the wound but it looked "rather more gangrenous than might be desired."

At noon the next day the wound haemorrhaged, bleeding "for some time before the alarm was given." Pressure and a tourniquet stopped it, but there was no thought of giving a transfusion. This new and highly suspect practice killed as many patients as it saved, because blood types were still unclassified. Harris failed rapidly now, despite regular doses of brandy and beef juice. "In spite of everything that could be done," the hospital report concluded, "he gradually sank until at 8:25 next morning he died, apparently from asthenia."

a cast-iron constitution

Asthenia, meaning weakness or debility, was often the "apparent" cause of death in the seventies. Doctors didn't really know why so many patients succumbed to simple surgery. Even so, the surgeon's knife wasn't as lethal as consumption, whooping cough, diphtheria or typhoid. Smallpox still killed hundreds each year because many families and even a few doctors distrusted vaccination. Nor did anyone understand the relative values of food. Malnutrition and indigestion were common; the latter was treated with violent purges. Indeed, the sulphur-and-molasses purge was rammed down children's throats every spring and autumn on general principles. It took luck and a cast-iron constitution for a child to reach school age. Simple sanitation, such as sterilization of babies' feeding bottles, was unknown; the rubber nipples with their sediment of stale caked milk were death traps. In 1870 nearly half of the forty-seven thousand deaths in Canada were children under five; fourteen thousand died in their first year.

ten thousand outdoor privies

The wonder was that *anyone* survived. Most drinking water came direct and unpurified from its source, which in cities generally meant from the same river that received raw sewage from towns upstream. It was far safer to drink rainwater or use private wells. A sample of Montreal's water, when analyzed in 1870, showed "animal and vegetable refuse, manure, fish spawn, straw, hayseed and a small cistoid worm." Ottawa, although admitting that pollution might plague some future generation, boasted that its sewage was "but a drop in the mighty waters of the Ottawa."

However, the installation of sewage systems never kept up with population growth and much of every city's waste stayed aromatically at home. Toronto's ten thousand outdoor privies, complained the *Sanitary Journal,* filled the summer skies with "air pollution." Even those affluent people with mahogany indoor "closets" (germ-laden, smelly but much admired as furniture) generally dug the contents into the back garden. Ordinary householders also tossed their slops outdoors and used garbage to level holes in the yard. Only the wealthy had private cesspools – holes where refuse drained into the ground but not, one hoped, into the well.

Bathtubs and baths were also a luxury, or an

eccentricity, of the rich. Builders didn't bother putting bathrooms in new houses; there was no demand. It would be nice, the *Sanitary Journal* said wistfully in 1874, if "bathing the entire body instead of just washing the face would become universal." Five years later it was still pleading: "If every man and woman in Canada could be induced every morning to take a cool bath, as cool as the system or constitution would bear – a sponge bath, say, a wash all over – it would impart such life and vigour into the people as to give a greater stimulus to work and business than could be given by the best legislation in the world."

The people, snug in sweaty flannel underwear, were deaf to such pleas. Why bathe when everything else was so dirty? Dust was so thick on the streets of Montreal that scores of people had chronic eye trouble. Toronto bakers' bread was a "dark mottled doughy mess" full of grit and scraps of fingernails. There was no milk or food inspection. Cheap candy often contained poisonous colouring material and ingredients such as plaster-of-Paris. Houses, with every crack sealed against the winter, reeked of unemptied chamber pots. Bed-bugs and lice were taken for granted even in some of the best homes.

a challenge for doctors

It was a challenge for Canada's three thousand registered doctors and few of them were up to it. The country had a dozen medical schools but facilities were as limited as the knowledge. In most, for example, there was a shortage of cadavers for classroom study. Canada's Anatomy Act provided that unclaimed bodies of paupers be turned over to medical science. Toronto, which generously gave away tons of bread and gallons of soup, drew charity cases from miles around and so never lacked for corpses. In other teaching centres, medical students had to rob graves by night.

What did the microbiologist see? The inset artist's sketch represents a microscopic view of city water that horrified readers of the Canadian Illustrated News *in 1870.*

Aspiring doctors, third-year medical students at the University of Toronto took a serious view of their future responsibilities.

With little training and almost no contact with new developments in their profession, rural doctors in particular were a poor bet. One immigrant complained:

When they hear a man's teeth chattering like a hundred pairs of castanets, they guess he has a fever and ague and administer quinine. When a patient complains of a pain in his heart they guess he has eaten too much fat pork and fixin's and give him a big pill. When an ailment is not of the ordinary backwoods type their diagnosis is mere guesswork. Backwoods ailments are seldom very complicated. They generally yield to simple remedies. It is only when the doctor begins prescribing his powders and draughts that there is any real danger.

A doctor was nevertheless well-rewarded for his and the patient's pains. As the July 1873 Toronto practitioners' official scale showed, the profession charged all the traffic would bear. Fees were levied according to the "presumed income of the patient" (first division patient, $3,000-plus; second division, $1,000 to $3,000; third division, under $1,000). Within each category a further spread allowed for "importance of case and circumstances of patient." Thus, a doctor with a gilt-edged patient charged $4 for a day call and double for nights; $10 for advice by mail; $6 for an office consultation. A doctor's attendance at childbirth cost poor people $6 to $10, the middle class $10 to $20, and the wealthy $20 to $50. Fees doubled for an instrument delivery.

almanacs and home remedies

What with the high fees and sheer peril, many Canadians preferred to doctor themselves with remedies from almanacs, home medical books or grandmother. There were dozens of cough cures – from resin in hot water to a heady mixture of

The Great Physician

William Osler, born in Bond Head, Ontario, completed his studies at McGill University (below) in 1872 at the age of twenty-three. Within two years he was on staff and affiliated with Montreal General Hospital. One of the leading pathologists of his time, a prolific and literate speaker and writer (noted for his text *Principles and Practice of Medicine*), he became renowned internationally as the great teaching physician of the late nineteenth century.

liquorice, vinegar, oil of almonds and tincture of opium. Children with croup got a poultice of mashed roast onions and hot goose or skunk oil. One remedy for acne was fine sand, rubbed wet on the face, then sponged off. Another was acid nitrate of mercury which "does not leave larger scars than the spots themselves would do." Honey, painted on two or three times a day, was said to prevent pitting in smallpox. A spider web applied to cuts stopped bleeding. And for sprains, strains, lame back and rheumatism, there was nothing like toad ointment, made by boiling four good-sized toads with fresh butter and tincture of arnica.

the young girl's plight

As if acne and croup weren't enough of a worry, parents of the seventies, like parents throughout history, were convinced that their children were headed for ruin in other ways, most of them having to do with the embarrassing human body. Adolescent boys were alarmingly interested in sex. Girls were getting so listless and rundown from corsets that crushed their lungs and underclothes slung from the waist instead of the shoulders that there wouldn't be any mothers left for the next generation. As a clergyman cried passionately to a fellow train passenger one day, "What can be done to save our young women?"

Puberty was a puzzling time for doctors and parents, but no more than it was for the kids. Sex, known among many adults as the "nameless sin," was never discussed in parent-child talks. Yet the grown-ups prescribed only one worthy career for a girl: motherhood. "Healthy bouncing girls with good digestion, hearty laugh, energetic and sprightly walk," enthused the *Canada Lancet* in 1879, "those who are never ill when they can help it and then only for good reason, are the women we want to be the future mothers of our race."

But some women aspired to careers. A woman

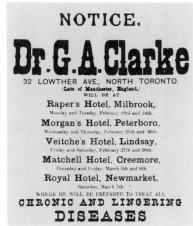

The itinerant Dr. Clarke boasted cures for chronic and lingering diseases, with "particular attention given to Female Complaints."

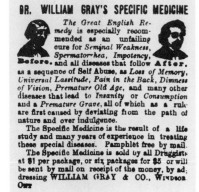

Dr. Gray's medicine was specifically for unmentionable Male Ailments.

writer had the audacity to discuss the young girl's plight in a *Canadian Illustrated News* article of 1873:

Who is so lost for something to do as the girl who has just left school? She has no occupations but a narrow circle of amusements and what becomes to her almost a duty – the perusal of the latest novel. She settles down to her narrow life, waiting for marriage to give her new thoughts and objects with which to interest herself.

The *Sanitary Journal* wrestled with this incredible thought. It was possible that girls might attain "the rank and intellectuality of boys. While it is true they have a smaller brain, it may be of a higher degree of organization. It is well known that the quality of the brain and its degree of organization are of great value in estimating intellectual ability. . . . A small brain may be very well organized and show more than average ability." But alas, there was a serious roadblock to higher education for girls. It was a distasteful one and the *Journal* handled it gingerly: "If it were possible to complete the education of boys and girls at the age of 13 or 14 or before that period in which nature develops the peculiarity of each sex, there could not probably be any arguments put forward against coeducation, from the sanitary standpoint. . . . But the excitement to which coeducation naturally gives rise is physically injurious."

sin and innocence

There was that old devil, sex, again. The less youngsters knew about it, the better. Nobody seemed to question how a girl could become a good mother of the race without learning a few basic facts of motherhood. This would all come in good time, the parents believed. Through puberty and the teens, the rule was: keep them busy and maybe

A Lady's Wardrobe

Completely covered from head to toe on most social occasions, women of
the 1870s bared their arms only for the beach. Walking dresses, sacques
and panniers reflect the emergence of the bustle – a frame or padding
worn to distend the fullness of the back of a woman's skirt. By 1875
this protuberance made it almost impossible for women to sit down.

Theatre playbills carried these ads.

they'll work off those unfortunate stirrings within them. Boys with acne were advised to "use a cold bath every morning, take plenty of exercise and be cautioned in reference to sexual matters." Young people were briskly hustled past nude statues and paintings. Early thoughts of sex, it was believed, were unhealthy as well as immoral.

sex as usual

"Youth, it cannot be too often repeated, is the time for storing strength, both physical and moral," warned the *Sanitary Journal*. "Among the passions of the future man, which at this period should be strictly reminded, is that of physical love; for none wars so completely against the principles which have been laid down as the most conducive to long life; no excess so thoroughly lessens the sum of the vital power; none so much weakens and softens the organs of life; none is more active in hastening vital consumption."

Sex existed, there was no denying, but nice people didn't talk about it. Anyone in search of guidance had to find it, scrap by scrap, on privy walls, in home health books, from knowledgeable older men and women, or in an awkward little talk with a doctor. From these sources a newcomer to the game might discover that sex after marriage was permissible, although one home health book warned against intercourse for three months after childbirth because it might dry up the mother's milk. A few doctors were even urging young brides to avoid exhausting "bridal journeys" and save their strength for the ardours ahead: "At this period a good constitution is needed to stand the excitement of love . . . when the uterus and its appendages are congested."

Premarital sex, however, was deemed sinful and unhealthy. Young men were warned that youthful sex would destroy the vigour of later life. *Canada Lancet* in 1871 spoke sternly of the

nation's "social evil" (bawdy houses) but added that closing them would merely drive "strumpets" into respectable homes as hired help "where their lewdness and evil influence may be exerted on the minds of hitherto innocent youths of both sexes."

Despite all these road blocks, sex went on more or less as usual, with the usual consequences. Since contraceptives were not sold publicly or discussed in print, women had to choose between ingenuity or pregnancy. Some made their own suppositories of moss, cotton wool or a combination of zinc, cocoa butter, henbane and almond oil. Some men employed a rubber sheath or a sheep-gut softened and dressed with almond oil. But birth control was far from foolproof, there were many unwanted pregnancies, in and out of wedlock, and many abortions, aided by pills sold in most drugstores but cleverly disguised as cures for female irregularities. No law prevented their sale any more than the sale of unmarked poisons.

the life-crushing waist

Yet doctors, churchmen and female crusaders avoided such unpleasant subjects and attacked, instead, a greater health "evil": women's clothing. "Wife and Mother," a tireless writer of letters to editors, summed it up in 1877: "Is the small disproportioned life-crushing waist beautiful? Is the woman graceful, tilted forward on high-heeled boots with hips thrown back to maintain her equilibrium? Or with hands in a muff and shoulders forced forward on the walls of the chest, impeding the action of the lungs? Or with one hand behind the other supporting her mud-bedraggled skirts and the opposite shoulder 'leading off in advance'?"

Graceful she was not. But two years later the Queen City Suspender Company of Cincinnati, Ohio, came to her rescue. The *Canadian Medical Record* hailed the glad news: "Our attention has

108

been called to a new article for the use of ladies which has conferred an everlasting blessing upon every lady. We refer to the Queen City Skirt Suspenders for supporting ladies' skirts. . . . These suspenders are recommended by our physicians to all ladies and young girls."

For all the obsession with ladies' suspenders, a few doctors were dealing with such urgent puzzles as mental health. Not many years before, all mental patients had been locked up in cells as a matter of principle. By the late seventies – although mental hospitals were still called "insane asylums" and the inmates "crazy people" – patients in such up-to-date quarters as the Ontario Asylum were well fed, free to roam within their wards and entertained with concerts. Mild forms of mania were now regarded as curable illness, although rest and quiet was the only treatment. There was even a groping awareness that emotional upset or exhaustion caused physical ills. In prescribing rest before meals, *Canada Sunday Magazine* added, "This is of the utmost importance to the businessman or person engaged in brain labour. Its violation is one of the chief causes of our national dyspepsia."

People of vision and science could see the pinpoint lights of change. In 1871 Dr. William Bayard, president of the New Brunswick Medical Society reviewed for his confrères how far their profession had come: Lister's interesting though untried theories; experimental skin transplants in Paris; medicine's new awareness of tumors, bronchitis, emphysema; new instruments such as the ophthalmoscope which helped see into the eye.

Gone were the days, he reminded them, when every doctor "bled" his patient on principle; when cauterization served for sutures and "the cries of the suffering were exceeded only by the hissing of heated iron against bleeding wound. Perhaps 60 or 70 years hence, the same may be said of those diseases that are at present the most destructive and deadly – consumption, convulsions, typhus, pneumonia. And who can say that means may not be devised to arrest the ravages of scarlet fever and whooping cough?"

His older colleagues exchanged indulgent smiles. A good man, young Bayard, but he had this bad habit of dreaming the impossible.

Corsets - lighter and tighter than whalebone - for women and girls.

Long before the days of Ivory - Lily White Soap. It floats!

Season's Greetings

Coming fast on the heels of the colourful trade cards and penny postcards of the decade, Christmas cards began to flood into Canadian homes. Artists adapted the photographic style of the day - the stiff poses and meticulously arranged composites of Wm. Notman can be recognized in some of the designs on these pages.

Wishing you a happy Christmas.

Toboggans and snowshoes dominated the design of Canadian cards.

Merry Christmas

The Frost look'd forth one still clear night,
And whisper'd "Now I shall be out of sight:
So, through the valley, and over the height,
In silence I'll take my way.
I will not go on like that blustering train –
The Wind and the Snow, the Hail and the Rain,
Who make so much bustle and noise in vain;
But I'll be as busy as they."

Then he flew to the mountain, and powdered its crest,
He lit on the trees, and their boughs he drest
In diamond beads; and, over the breast
Of the quivering lake, he spread
A coat of mail, that it need not fear
The glitt'ring point of many a spear,
Which he hung on its margin, far and near,
Where a rock could rear its head.

He went to the window of those who slept,
And over each pane, like a fairy, crept;
Wherever he breathed, wherever he stept,
By the light of the moon, were seen—
Most beautiful things "There were flow'rs and trees,
There were bevies of birds, and swarms of bees,
There were cities with temples, and tow'rs – and these,
All pictured in silvery sheen!

He peeped in the cupboard, and there was a sight
That changed him into a mischievous sprite,
For, as Christmas came with the morning light,
The place had been fill'd with good cheer.
He bit a basket of fruit on the shelf,
The wine bottles burst, and he helped himself,
Wishing everyone, as he drank their health,
"Merry Christmas and Happy New Year!"

The Merry Christmas adventures of Jack Frost were the subject of this card.

Publisher J.T. Henderson's New Year's card based on Notman's composite.

Gallant gentlemen alone made the wintry calls, bearing New Year's greetings.

A giant lobster, a skating bear and Uncle Sam in "The Masquerade."

Winter vignettes were intricately worked into this variation on a theme.

CHAPTER TEN

Home, Sweet Home

Success in housekeeping adds. . . lustre to a woman's accomplishments.

The Canadian Home Cook Book, 1877

Whether it was a sod hut, log shanty, whitewashed plaster cottage or shack of siding and tarpaper, a home of one's own was the goal of every Canadian. Paying off and keeping it was every man's ideal. Mortgaging or selling it was a tragedy. No one dreamed of leaving it after retirement. Homes were passed on to the children who were born in them, so they too could live and die there, and will the property to their children. Home was security, success, a place to be crammed with all the precious clutter of one's life.

The nesting instinct even infected bachelors, boarding in their single rooms at $3 or $5 a week. Canada's first recorded do-it-yourself addict was an anonymous young man of the seventies "who had but $25 to furnish his room and made such a den that no one could enter it without envying him!" Upon renting the bare room he immediately took down the "commonplace marble mantel," built another of pine, painted it black and the brick dark red, and put up inexpensive andirons. He calcimined the walls "Pompeiian red," made a dado of olive-green wallpaper and hung a frieze of Japanese fans.

Next he stained the floor dark brown for sixty cents, laid an "exceedingly pretty" seven-dollar rug and hung curtains of dark brown Canton flannel (twelve cents a yard) on black curtain poles. Eight dollars bought a second-hand cabinet and mahogany table. He polished them with linseed oil, pumice and an old felt hat, then covered this handiwork with more flannel. Over the mantel went an old-fashioned mirror (gift from grandmother) with peacock feathers arranged around it. Up went brass candlesticks (grandma again), engravings, more Japanese fans and Japanese vases. He prettied up three battered chairs (fifty cents apiece) with black and gold paint. Once more to the Orient for a pink Japanese umbrella, hung handle-up to make a shade for an ugly gaslight fixture. With a few potted plants, the place was finished.

Not many, single or married, had such a flair for decoration – or such a kindly grandmother. Fewer still had the crystal chandeliers, carpets thick as prairie grass, velvet drapes or full-length mirrors of certain Montreal financiers. But all of them lavished love, in their various ways, on home.

What was a typical middle class home? Well. . . . It is 6:45 A.M. on November 10, 1879. We are entering a narrow two-storey red brick Toronto house, with verandah, weathervane, attic and gingerbread trim dripping and writhing from every gable. Here lives a forty-year-old bank accountant, his wife, three children and Maggie, the Irish

LUCY : " Isn't he handsome ? Isn't he a love ? "
HETTY : " What a comfort he must be to his mother,—he is *so* sweet
LUCY : " Wouldn't I like to kiss him for his mother !

Grinchuckle, *a Montreal humour magazine, pokes gentle fun at the young ladies' sole ambition - to charm a man into marriage.*

Opposite page: Girls were trained early in the domestic crafts. A twelve-year-old laboriously worked this needle-point sampler from 1870.

This young lad, with hair neatly parted in the middle, shows off his braid and velvet suit, white stockings and Mary Jane shoes, while posing with Mother and Father.

girl-of-all-work. This solid citizen, earning $932 a year after twenty years of faithful toil, is slowly but stubbornly paying off his mortgage. None of his possessions, with the possible exception of his family, means so much.

His wife, worn and matronly at twenty-nine, is already up and supervising Maggie. Home is this wife's domain, the one area where she is totally in charge. Her kitchen, small and dark but well equipped with tall cupboard for pots, pans, dishes and earthen crocks, is more convenient than the old-fashioned basement kitchen many houses still have. Lugging a heaping meal upstairs, three times a day, drives many a maid to other employment.

The pride of this kitchen is the wood-and-coal-burning range, a mighty black monster with fire-box, oven, four lids, a reservoir for heating water and an abundance of iron curlicue trim. Its pipes, running through the second storey to a chimney, help warm the upstairs. Already Maggie, who sleeps in a tiny room off the kitchen, has performed the morning ritual of removing ashes, re-stoking the fire and shining the monster's face with lard.

miniature adults

Upstairs, husband and children are dressing and splashing cold water on their faces from bedroom basins. The small boys are pulling on floppy pantalets, hateful high boots and blouses made by women's dressmakers. The daughter is clad in a miniature version of Mama's dress. Maggie carries up a pitcher of hot water for the Mister's shave. Upstairs there are three bedrooms, and a cubicle for the "earth closet" toilet (a handsome mahogany-encased structure with pan of earth under the seat). There is talk of a sewage system reaching this part of town soon but at present waste water is tossed out back and excrement is dug into the garden.

But there's a good water system: a brick cistern which catches rainfall for wash water, and a well to provide drinking water. Both can be drawn on at will by a marvel of modern engineering, a kitchen pump with two stop cocks and two lead pipes leading to the sources. There is no bathroom: baths are a Saturday-night ritual in a tub beside the range.

a new awareness

Breakfast is a substantial spread of hominy, molasses, toast, jam, mutton chops, fried potatoes and tea. By eight o'clock, husband and children are off to work and school. While Maggie washes the dishes in the dry sink (no drain) and makes beds, the housewife answers the door, over and over. Iceman with his daily delivery. Baker's cart. Messenger with what seems to be an invitation (Mr. Bell's new telephone has not yet reached this home) but the envelope is addressed to both her and her husband so she saves it for him. Postman with a letter from Mama in Hamilton and the latest *Canadian Illustrated News.*

For one idle moment she pauses to flick through the *News,* admiring its large graphic sketches of current events and its advertisements. "Gray's Syrup of Red Spruce Gum for coughs." Must try that for the children. "The Cook's Friend Baking Powder has become a household word in the land and is a household necessity." She'll be using some this very afternoon. A news item, "The General Evil," tells how young girls leave school and neglect to acquire further knowledge of the really important thing in life: being a wife and mother. How true! Young girls no longer take marriage seriously.

The gilt and onyx clock in the parlour says nine. Time to start Maggie on the Monday wash. Washing is no longer the awful soak-on-Monday-scrub-on-Tuesday ordeal. The new patent washer

Energy-conscious G.H. Pedlar patented this Fuel Saver in October 1871.

A Voice on the Wire

The nation that today makes the greatest number of telephone calls of any in the world defiantly claims to be the birthplace of the telephone. Alexander Graham Bell *did* emigrate from Scotland to Canada with his parents in 1870, but it was his work at the Boston School for the Deaf that provided the basis for his technological breakthrough in transmitting the human voice over a wire.

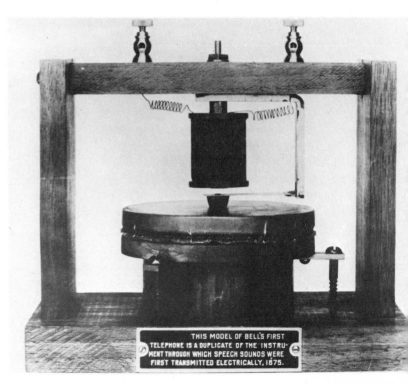

THIS MODEL OF BELL'S FIRST TELEPHONE IS A DUPLICATE OF THE INSTRUMENT THROUGH WHICH SPEECH SOUNDS WERE FIRST TRANSMITTED ELECTRICALLY, 1875.

Above: A model of Bell's telephone first used in June 1875, in Boston, Mass.

Alexander Graham Bell (left), aged 29 in 1876, the year of the telephone.

amilton, Ontario, opened the first telephone
xchange in the British Empire in July 1878.

*A transmitter-receiver box for hand telephone.
These first commercial ones were used in 1877.*

*Bell made the first long-distance call from
Brantford to Paris, Ont., using this receiver.*

vrille Duquet of Quebec patented the first
mbined hand telephone in 1878.

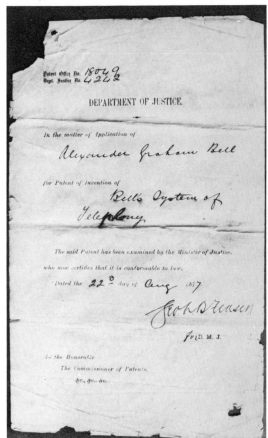

Patent Office No. 18049
Dept. Justice No. 4242

DEPARTMENT OF JUSTICE.

In the matter of Application of

Alexander Graham Bell

for Patent of invention of

Bells System of
Telephony

The said Patent has been examined by the Minister of Justice,
who now certifies that it is conformable to law.

Dated the 22ᵈ day of Aug 1877

*Note the commissioner's uncertainty about the
spelling of the unfamiliar word "telephony."*

*With this model of 1879, the caller no longer
moved the instrument from mouth to ear.*

The one-room schoolhouse welcomed scholars of all ages like this group posing with their school marms in Oxford County.

William Kirby
Poet and Novelist

In 1877, former Niagara *Mail* editor and customs collector, William Kirby published his novel, *The Golden Dog,* a vivid picture of the days of Montcalm and New France. Quebec poet, Louis Fréchette translated it and, in all, the book went through some thirty editions. The author lived to be eighty-nine, publishing other historical sketches and long patriotic poems, but this novel remained his most popular work.

tumbles the clothes by a clever series of gears connected to a push-pull handle run by Maggie-power. Many women now buy bar soap and whittle the shavings into the wash water. But this housewife thriftily makes her own from quicklime, washing soda, fat and resin.

In two hours the wash is on the line. Meanwhile the wife has cleaned the coal-oil lamps, a delicate task never entrusted to thick-fingered Maggie: fragile glass chimneys washed and dried, wicks evenly trimmed, glass base refilled. There are gaslight fixtures in parlour and dining room but for kitchen and bedroom and for reading the family still depends on lamps.

Now, while Maggie prepares a huge hot dinner for noon, the housewife dusts the parlour. This dismal room, used only on occasions of high state, is darkened by heavy drapes and dull wallpaper of a huge floral pattern – and she adores it. The carpet is brown, also with a floral design. The fireplace has a high mantel and small iron grate. Everywhere are furniture and knick knacks: fat

hassocks, hefty walnut chairs, firescreen, the walnut whatnot (a series of shelves on spool-turned supports, harbouring all kinds of treasures). There are gilt ornaments, china ornaments, a brass-bound album of mementos and pressed flowers, a family Bible, hard beadwork cushions and a prized photograph of a cousin in Montreal, taken by the famous Mr. Notman. The cousin stands with frozen stare, hand on hip and one foot crossed over the other in studied casualness. He looks as though he is supported by hidden props which, in fact, he *was* during the long slow exposure.

Dinner is set out on the massive mahogany table. The family pulls up in heavy mahogany chairs; heads are bowed in grace; then the meal proceeds to the accompaniment of dignified small-talk, the children joining in only with father's permission. Afterward, the wife eagerly produces the invitation. Her husband smooths his greying mutton-chop whiskers and gravely opens it. What an incredible honour! The managing director of the bank requests the pleasure of their company

118

In the seventies, higher education was only for the sons of the well-to-do at institutions like University College.

for an "at home" on Sunday afternoon next. Such an invitation has never come before. Could it possibly indicate a promotion – oh, not *now* but perhaps in a year or so?

She tackles her afternoon chores with new delight. Maggie, having fired up the oven, is testing it with her arm. (The heat becomes more than she can bear at the count of 35; just about right for a cake.) Meanwhile, her mistress mixes bread dough, to be left to rise overnight. Bread-making is one of her pleasures; the symmetrical crusty dark loaves are a joy to the eye as well as to the palate.

Maggie begins the ironing, a tedious job, three flat-irons heating on the kitchen range while she uses the fourth, skilfully testing it now and then with the *sssss* of a moistened fingertip. The housewife brings out her sewing basket. There is always needlework, not the ordinary mending which Maggie does, but decorative embroidering, beading, crocheting, tatting: dress and handkerchief trimming, doilies, mats, jackets for fishbowls, chair covers, pincushions, pillow cases, and antimacassars as well as wall protectors to keep greasy male heads from staining the wallpaper.

Crazywork is the rage just now: assorted shapes, sizes, kinds and colours of material joined with different colours of embroidery silk to make covers for a pillow, chair, table or bed. Some of the designs are amazing. A magazine recently told of a crazywork spread that brought $150 at a fall fair, having for its centrepiece a needlework Oscar Wilde "in aesthetic costume with a lily in one hand and the orthodox sunflower in the other." If a woman runs out of needlework there is always decalcomanie, the popular new technique of putting designs on crockery, glass, even clothes by means of transfers.

Supper is over. The children are asleep. Maggie, having washed the last dish and privately grumbled that a girl really earns her $7 a month around this house, has fallen into bed. Now, around the dining-room lamp, the invitation must be properly answered. The young wife watches

William Francis Butler
Officer and Travel Writer

William Francis Butler's two books on his travels in the North-West, *The Great Lone Land* (1872) and *The Wild North Land* (1873) are classics of the period. An adventurous British Army captain, Butler served as an intelligence officer in the Red River Expedition of 1870. Then he made the two extensive journeys recounted in his books – the first on the Saskatchewan River across the prairies, and the second to Lake Athabasca and into British Columbia. Butler left Canada in 1873, continuing his service in other parts of the British Empire.

119

Charlotte Nickinson and Father
A Family of the Stage

"Charlotte Nickinson, born in 1832, early showed her talent for the stage. Her father, Major John Nickinson, also an eminent actor, became the lessee of the Royal Lyceum at Toronto, and at that house she was the leading lady up to her marriage with David Morrison, a journalist, in 1858. After her husband's death in 1870, she assumed the management of the Grand Opera House in Toronto, and maintained her reputation as a talented and sterling actress for several seasons."

from *Types of Canadian Women*

proudly while her husband composes a reply in his heavy Spencerian script: ". . . have much pleasure in accepting your kind invitation." His penmanship is impeccable, and so it should be. Good writing is the first requisite of a man in business. A sample of his "hand" was the first thing the bank requested, years ago.

With the reply dried and sealed, he picks up the daily *Globe*. His wife looks guiltily at the sewing basket. But tonight, exhilarated by the invitation, she reaches instead for a back issue of *Belford's Magazine,* saved for such a frivolous moment, and picks up the threads of a serial:

. . . Her doctor entered. I looked at him anxiously. He looked grave. I took him aside. "There is no hope," he said at last, in answer to my urgent question. "She has sustained severe internal injuries. She may go at any moment."

I heard as if in a dream. She, go! My love! My northern bird! My lady of the rose-leaf-lips! My life!

At this moment she came to herself and said, "It is better so." As though she felt the fatal moment to be near she said with an effort, feebly motioning with her head toward the door, "Send him away – you – alone – confess."

The doctor left the room. She whispered. I bent over her. "Forgive your darling . . ." The words came with difficulty now ". . . but – I – am – married!"

She rose up in her bed. Something came to her lips. In a moment the white sheet was stained with blood. She fell back with a sigh. She was dead.

With a loud cry I rushed to the door to call the doctor back. My brain reeled. I fell heavily to the ground. I remembered nothing more.

Our housewife puts aside her magazine and stares misty-eyed into the yellow flame. It was wicked for lady-of-the-rose-leaf-lips to fall in love while married, of course. And yet, poor thing – what sadness some people have! How lucky to have a fine home and successful husband! She glances fondly at him, feeling for one wicked moment a long-forgotten excitement. How delicious if he were to sweep her into his arms and carry her upstairs . . . .

But he is deep in the news of November 10, 1879. The steamship *Arizona* has been struck by an iceberg off Halifax. R.J. Hunter of King Street offers $18 suits. Gold has been found at Rainy River. Cale's shop is selling celluloid shirt collars and perforated buckskin underwear. Professor Macoun reports a great coal deposit in the Northwest, south of Battleford, and adds that the prairie Indians, although starving, are not hostile. J.D. Nasmith at Jarvis and Adelaide now offers fresh crumpets every afternoon. Many train wrecks in the United States. Mighty England is "demanding" that Turkey reform her government. Tenders are being called for construction of the Canadian Pacific Railway.

Her husband yawns, consults his pocket watch and leads the way upstairs to bed. *How fortunate are we to be part of the Empire! What a prosperous growing land this Canada is becoming! And, best of all, how good it is to be home.*

The First Edition

of the *Canadian Illustrated News* came off the press in October 1869. Until its demise in 1883, the magazine provided Canada-wide coverage by reporters and artists of all political and social events of the age of innocence. Its line drawings and the first photographic reproductions remain today an invaluable portrait of daily life in the Canada of the seventies.

Canadian Illustrated News

VOL. I.—No. 1.]   MONTREAL, SATURDAY, OCTOBER 30, 1869.   [SINGLE COPIES, TEN CENTS. $4 PER YEAR IN ADVANCE.

H. R. H. PRINCE ARTHUR. From a Photograph by Notman.—See Page 6.

George E. Desbarats, born in Quebec in 1838, followed long-standing family tradition into the printing and publishing field. His most noteworthy ventures were the magazines, the Canadian Illustrated News *(above) and* L'Opinion Publique *(page 86).*

Temperature in the shade, and Barometer indications for the week ending Tuesday, 28th May, 1872, observed by Hearn, Harrison & Co., 242 & 244 Notre Dame Street.

		Max.	Min.	Mean.	8 a.m.	1 p.m.	6 p.m.
W.,	May 22.	71°	49°	60°	30.00	30.02	29.94
Th.,	" 23.	65°	53°5	59°2	29.65	29.70	29.80
Fri.,	" 24.	63°	48°5	55°7	29.90	29.85	29. 2
Sat.,	" 25.	63°	53°	58°	29.76	29.76	29.80
Su.,	" 26.	70°	54°	62°	29.95	30.00	29.95
M.,	" 27.	66°	51°	58°5	29.85	29.75	29.70
Tu.,	" 28.	64°	53°5	58°	29.67	29.73	29.90

Our readers are reminded that the subscription to the News is $4.00 per annum, **PAYABLE IN ADVANCE.**

All unpaid subscribers will be struck off the list on the 1st July next, and their accounts [at the rate of $5.00 per annum] placed in our attorneys' hands for collection.

ROUND THE WORLD.

Samuel J. Randall, of Pennsylvania, has been elected Speaker of the United States House of Representatives.

A new Cabinet has been formed at Athens, the late Ministry having been defeated on the question of war taxes.

Mr. Gladstone has renewed his attack on Lord Beaconsfield and his Eastern policy, holding him personally responsible for the present position of the Government.

Although hopes are expressed in Constantinople of the Conference having a peaceful issue, Turkish commanders have received orders to provision the Danube fortresses for eight months.

HUMOROUS.

Three-year-old happened to have a want to be attended to just as his mother was busy with the baby.

"Go away; I can't be bothered with you now."

"What did you have so many children for, if you can't bother with 'em?" he unexpectedly inquired.

George Francis Train says he has "sunk his egotism in the universal." Nothing short of the universal would hold it.

THE YOUNG CANADIAN MECHANIC.—From a Sketch by Jas. McDonald, Collingwood, Ont.

THE TELEPHONE OUTDONE!

STARTLING STRIDE OF CIVILIZATION—A WILD DREAMER'S DREAM — THE TELEOPTISCOPE WHICH REPRODUCES BY TELEGRAPH A PERFECT IMAGE OF A PERSON OR OBJECT THOUSANDS OF MILES AWAY.

And the professor resumed the languid and meditative manipulation of his post-prandial toothpick; while the *Bulletin* reporter, to whom this oracular prophecy was addressed by his eccentric friend, in a corner of their accustomed dining place, encouragingly responded:

"But you don't really look for any new stride, immediately, do you? Civilization advances, not steadily, but by jumps, and at long intervals. But it's scarcely a year since the telephone was first talked of."

"Yes, to tell the truth, I do," was the hesitating answer; "and I rather hope to point the way myself."

"Do tell a fellow."

"Well, there can't be any harm now, I s'pose, though it is not quite perfect. I don't know as I care to profit pecuniarily by the invention myself; but I do want the honour of it. I must complete it alone. I can't divide the work with any pirate. However, I can tell you the general object and method without revealing the unperfected secrets of it."

"Good fellow! Go on! I'm all attention."

"I believe that the telegraph wire can be made to transmit light as well as sound; that we can devise apparatus that will produce, at a distance of hundreds of thousands of miles, a perfect eidolon——"

"Eidolon? What is an eidolon?"

"Well, an image then. A perfect image of any person or object. We shall be able to see as well as hear our friends, no matter how far away. Distances will be practically annihilated."

Courtesy forbade any expression of the listener's incredulity; but he could not repress a smile.

"You may laugh! He laughs best who laughs at last! The theory is very simple, though, after all.

"Light is only one form of force. So is sound; so is heat; so is electricity. If the vibrations of the one can be conducted by solids for any distance—that is, if a molecular motion can be started at one end of a wire by one of them, which is transmitted to the other, and is there appreciable—so can another. And——"

"Hold a minute," said the reporter, who was an amateur scientist himself.

"You must remember that there are good and bad conductors of electricity, good and bad conductors for heat, good and bad conductors for light. A telegraph wire may conduct the vibrations of electricity any distance; but light can't go through opaque matter a hundredth part of an inch. Besides, light can't turn a corner as electricity can."

"Not so fast! Suppose we do not transmit the same rays of light the whole distance, but make the vibrations given off by any object operate delicate telegraph keys, just as the vibrating diaphragm of the telephone does? See! The sound which comes out of a telephone, so to speak, is not the one that went into it, but one exactly like it. So with the image that will be conveyed by the Teleoptiscope."

Courrier des Dames.

Our lady readers are invited to contribute to this department.

MISTRESSES AND MAIDS; IS ANOTHER CONFERENCE NECESSARY?

Would those who advocate treating servants as equals look very pleasant if the footman who opens the door to their visitors was to follow them into the drawing-room and take his seat amongst them? Or if the cook, housemaid, and coachman, took their places with the family at the dinner table? And if they were permitted to do these things, which as equals they of course should do, would it add at all to the happiness and comfort of either family or servants? I think not. There is however something to be said on the other side. Some treat their servants, not as if they were their fellow-creatures, in an inferior position, but as if they were altogether an inferior class of beings, not made of the same flesh and blood as themselves and not having the same feelings. Others are unkind through mere thoughtlessness, often causing a servant to run up and down stairs two or three times, when by a little thought, what was required might have been done just as well at one time. Then, too, a kind word or a pleasant "thank you" will often make a tired servant feel less tired, or set her at her work again with a more cheerful and contented spirit. Let the ladies take a hint.

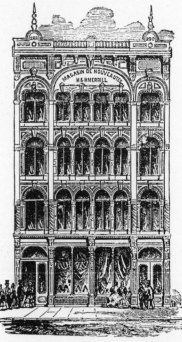

A BOY KILLED BY A HORSE.—At Hillsburg, David Simpson, aged thirteen years, son of Mr. John Simpson, East Garafraxa, was thrown from a horse and killed. The horse had the harness on him when the boy left for the field, and when found was standing a short distance from the boy with the collar and the rest of the harness stripped completely off him, and the boy lying quite dead.

SAVED FROM DESTRUCTION.—As the Great Western train was leaving the station at Hamilton, a young man evidently the worse of liquor was seen standing on the track. He would have inevitably been crushed by the engine, which was almost upon him, had not John Murray, porter of the Rossin House, seized him and pulled him off the track. Mr. Murray hurt his hand badly in so doing.

RECOVERY OF A STOLEN DOG.—A valuable dog, the property of Mr. J. A. Ouimet, M.P., was stolen recently from his premises in Montreal. Detective Lafon traced the animal to a barge lying at the wharf. On boarding the vessel the detective was met by a member of the crew, who demanded his business in a threatening manner. The sight of the detective's badge and a loaded revolver had a wondeful effect in quieting him, and the dog was speedily forthcoming.

A WARM RECEPTION.—The other night, as a gentleman well known in society, and noted, moreover, for his skill in the "noble art of self-defence," was going home up Drummond street, Montreal, he was attacked by two men, one of whom endeavoured to snatch his watch chain. They reckoned without their host, however, as their intended victim at once brought his pugilistic capabilities into play, and though the odds were against him, succeeded in inflicting severe punishment on the would-be highwaymen.

REMARKABLE ESCAPE OF A HORSE.—One day last week there was a good horse attached to an express waggon, belonging to Mr. Lapierre, merchant, standing in front of the Bonsecours Market, when it was frightened by a noise made by a man who had put himself outside too much liquor. The horse ran away towards the revetment wall, the railing surmounting which it endeavoured to jump. In the attempt, he slipped under the bars over the wall, and as the waggon was caught by the railing, he hung suspended by the traces. He was released without any damage being done.

Acknowledgements

Scores of books and hundreds of individual issues of newspapers and magazines helped steep me in the mood of the decade. To a few, I am particularly grateful for warm, lively, detailed accounts of how ordinary people lived. I admit, too, to receiving inspiration from certain ghosts: on a high plateau by the Red Deer River one silent morning, overlooking the site of Tail Creek Town; in the scrawled diary of a Toronto doctor of the seventies; in the heavy handwriting of some anonymous civil servant who recorded Strike Him on the Back's first treaty payment; and in the nineteenth century Toronto house where this book was written, overlooking King Street where Toronto workmen first marched for the nine-hour day.

I'm indebted as well, to the patient, unflappable librarians of the Toronto Central Reference Library, the Toronto City Hall Business Library, the Toronto Academy of Medicine and the Glenbow-Alberta Institute.

Most of all, I thank Floy and Jack Collins who long ago showed me, first-hand, the special courage of pioneers.

Robert Collins

The Author

Robert Collins was born and raised near Shamrock, Saskatchewan, and served for three years with the R.C.A.F. in Canada, England and Germany. His interest in journalism began with his work on military newspapers while overseas. Since graduating from the University of Western Ontario in 1950, he has written non-stop and worked as editor for various magazines, including *Maclean's, Imperial Oil Review, Toronto Life* and *Reader's Digest.* The author of six books— among them *A Great Way To Go: The Automobile in Canada, The History of Telecommunications,* and two books of fiction—and a contributor to three books on natural history, Robert Collins lives in Toronto.

Index

The page numbers in italics refer to illustrations and captions

Picture Credits

We would like to acknowledge the help and cooperation of the directors and staff of the various public institutions and the private firms and individuals who made available paintings, posters, mementoes, collections and albums as well as photographs and gave us permission to reproduce them. Every effort has been made to identify and credit appropriately the sources of all illustrations used in this book. Any further information will be appreciated and acknowledged in subsequent editions.

The illustrations are listed in the order of their appearance on the page, left to right, top to bottom. Principal sources are credited under these abbreviations:

EAT   Archives, Eaton's of Canada Limited
CIN   Canadian Illustrated News
GAF   Glenbow-Alberta Foundation
MTCL   Metropolitan Toronto Central Library
NPA   Notman Photographic Archives—
         McCord Museum, Montreal
OA   Ontario Archives
PABC   Provincial Archives of British Columbia
PAC   Public Archives of Canada

/1 GAF /2 Royal Canadian Mounted Police Museum, Regina, Saskatchewan /4 MTCL /6 PAC, C 18060 /7 GAF /8 MTCL /9 CIN /10 OA; NPA /11 Miller Services; PABC; CIN /12 PAC, C 14469 /13 PAC, L 4389 /14 NPA; PAC, C 9471 /15 Nova Scotia Museum; CIN, MTCL /16-17 All from NPA /18 NPA /19 Montreal Amateur Athletic Association /20 OA; OA /21 CIN /22 OA; A.F.M. Bell-Smith; CIN; Sports Hall of Fame, Canadian National Exhibition /23 Royal Canadian Yacht Club, Toronto; MTCL; *L'Opinion Publique*, Paul Duval; *Canadian Gentlemen's Journal*, OA /24 John Ross Robertson Collection, MTCL /25 Massey Ferguson Limited /26 Canadian Labour Congress /27 CIN /28 CIN /29 *Grip; Grip* /30 PAC, C 3833 /31 *Grinchuckle*; PAC, L 4396; PAC, C 5338 /32 NPA /33 OA /34 PAC, C 9210 /35 PAC; OA /36 PABC /37 PABC /38 University of British Columbia Library /39 CIN /40 PABC; PABC /41 PAC 51137; Smithsonian Institute, National Anthropological Archives; PABC /42 PABC /43 PABC /44 PABC /45 *My Canadian Journal,* Marchioness of Dufferin & Ava; PAC; PAC /46 GAF /47-48 All from Royal Canadian Mounted Police Museum, Regina, Saskatchewan /49 GAF; MTCL /50 Provincial Archives, Manitoba /51 GAF /52 Provincial Archives, Manitoba /53 GAF /54 PAC, C 14106 /55 Provincial Archives, Manitoba /56 PAC, C 7104 /57 GAF /58 Library of the Hudson's Bay Company /59 Private collection /60 EAT /61 PABC; OA; EAT; OA /62 Miller Services; Collection T. A. Reed, EAT /63 Simpson's /64 Simpson's /65 EAT; EAT /66 EAT; EAT; Private collection /67 Private collection; EAT; EAT; EAT; Private collection /68 Confederation Centre for the Arts, P.E.I. /69 PAC C 12815 /70 Norman Johnson /71 Public Archives of P.E.I., 2755 /72 OA; OA; NPA; CIN /73 OA; PAC, PA 22057; CIN /74 Public Archives of P.E.I., 2755; Confederation Centre for the Arts, P.E.I. /75 Harris paintings from Confederation Centre for the Arts, P.E.I.; Public Archives of P.E.I. /76 Archives of Saskatchewan /77 Fine Art Ephemera Collection, MTCL; Private collection; Private collection /78 Fine Art Ephemera Collection, MTCL; EAT /79 EAT; Fine Art Ephemera Collection, MTCL; MTCL; Private collection; MTCL /80 Photographer, H. de Jouvancourt, Private collection /81 NPA /82 All from CIN, MTCL /83 PAC C 23565 /84 CIN, PAC, C 14507; CIN, MTCL; *L'Opinion Publique* /85 United Church Archives /86 *L'Opinion Publique,* PAC, C 43905; *L'Opinion Publique,* MTCL /87 PAC, C 43711 /88 PAC, Topley 18887 /89-92 Massey Ferguson Limited /93 PAC, C 43678 /94 OA /95 CIN /96 Public Archives of P.E.I.; MTCL /97 Massey Ferguson Limited; OA /98 MTCL; CIN /99 PAC, SI 2774 /100-102 All from Academy of Medicine, Toronto /103 Academy of Medicine, Toronto; CIN, PAC C 24366 /104 OA /105 Private collection; CIN, MTCL /106 OA; OA /107 CIN, PAC C 14493 /108 OA /109 EAT; EAT; EAT /110 MTCL; Hallmark Historical Collection, William E. Coutts Company Limited; MTCL /111 MTCL; All others from the Hallmark Historical Collection, William E. Coutts Company Limited /112 Mr. & Mrs. J. Gibson /113 *Grinchuckle,* MTCL /114 MTCL /115 OA /116-117 Patent from PAC; All others from the Telephone Historical Collection, The Bell Telephone Company of Canada /118 University of Toronto Library; OA /119 CIN; Private collection /120 University of Toronto Library /121 CIN; NPA /122-124 CIN

1875

Railway survey of Newfoundland conducted by Sandford Fleming

Supreme Court of Canada established

Caraquet Riot in New Brunswick over separate schools issue

Riel begins five years of exile

Indian Treaty #5 with Swampy Cree and Chippewa

Forts Macleod, Walsh and Calgary established by N.W.M.P.

Construction of CPR transcontinental begins at Thunder Bay

First organized hockey in Victoria Rink, Montreal

Halifax *Herald* established

Icelanders establish settlement at Gimli, Manitoba

Pacific collides with *Orpheus* off B.C. coast; 250 lives lost

1876

Opposition leader John A. Macdonald formulates Conservatives' National Policy

North-West Territories Act; David Laird first lieutenant-governor

Indian Treaty #6 with Plains and Wood Cree

Intercolonial Railway officially completed from Ontario to Maritimes

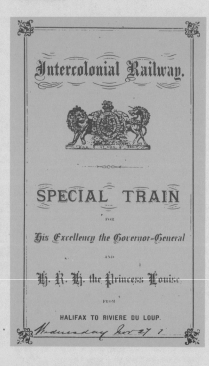

Toronto *Telegram* established by John Ross Robertson

Alexander Graham Bell completes first 'long distance' telephone call – Brantford to Paris, Ontario

Alexander Ewan builds first salmon cannery on Fraser River

Ned Hanlan wins U.S. Centennial single sculls.

First wheat harvest (Red Fife) in Manitoba to yield a surplus for export

First session of the Supreme Court of Canada

Montcalm and St. Hyacinthe fires in Quebec destroy 911 houses

1877

Indian Treaty #7 with Blackfoot

Dominion Fisheries Act

Charlottetown *Examiner* begins publication

Hanlan wins Canadian championship on Toronto Bay

University of Manitoba chartered

First McGill hockey club organized

Wm. Kirby publishes *The Golden Dog: "A Legend of Quebec"*